MW00779301

Immigrants and Change

Immigrants and Change

By

Roger Sherman

CAMBRIDGE SCHOLARS
P U B L I S H I N G

Immigrants and Change
By Roger Sherman

This book first published 2013

Cambridge Scholars Publishing

12 Back Chapman Street, Newcastle upon Tyne, NE6 2XX, UK

British Library Cataloguing in Publication Data
A catalogue record for this book is available from the British Library

ISBN (10): 1-4438-5240-6, ISBN (13): 978-1-4438-5240-1

TABLE OF CONTENTS

ABSTRACT

This text argues that a religious world view or a religious subcultural identity as expressed by the theory of Moral Cosmology is only one of many subcultural identities that the immigrant utilizes in their assimilation to a new host environment. It offers two alternative theories, a multiple subcultural identity formulation and the theory of inter-sectionality to explain changes in immigrant opinions as they transition from immigrant generation, to 1.5 to 2.0 generation. Relying upon data available through the General Social Survey (waves 2006, 2008, 2010), this study conducted a comparative analysis of the post1965 immigrant group and their expressed opinions on substantive issues of social and economic concerns to capture shifts in immigrant opinion. These opinion shifts are perceived as being driven by a multiplicity of salient subcultural identities implemented by the immigrant as tools to problem solve in the real world. Findings suggest that immigrant generational stage, gender and respondents self-identified religious tradition are more significant in the development of motivation and justification for the immigrant stances on substantive issues than a religious world view or respondent's religious orthodoxy. This study was unable to identify a significant linear correlation between religious orthodoxy and expressed opinions on substantive issues of social and economic concerns.

ACKNOWLEDGEMENTS

To the Annie E Casey Foundation whose financial support made this project possible.

To Carlos Forment whose critical reading of this work was essential.

To Pyong Gap Min whose mentorship instilled in me my curiosity about immigration.

To Andrew Arato for his guidance and continuous support during the many years I have labored on this life project.

To my wife Barbara and daughter Amanda, who have encouraged and supported me in too many ways to describe.

LIST OF TABLES

LIST OF PLOTS

CHAPTER ONE

INTRODUCTION

Main Objective

This text is about immigrants and changes they experience as they adjust to living in a new country. It is about theoretical explanations and how best to understand these changes. Most importantly it is a comparative intergenerational study of the post1965 new immigrant groups. How I came to write about the post1965 immigrant was a journey in itself. This study developed over time as an outgrowth of two significant albeit quite different socio-theoretical interests. The first being an interest in the political – theoretical tensions surrounding the first amendment issue of separation of church and state; in a liberal democracy should restraint be required in the use of religious thinking for political justification and the opposing position that religious arguments as justification for political opinions are legitimate justification for expressing opinions in the public sphere of civil society (Audi 1993).[1] I had initially thought to focus upon what should or should not be the basis of a citizen's political opinion cast in the public sphere. The analysis of opinion justification; what do citizens really think when it comes time to cast their opinion and is this process different for the immigrant citizen? I came to realize that the study I wanted to undertake was both less political in nature and broader in sociological scope, yet still addressing the issue of what lays beneath public opinion.

The second formative interest was my growing passion for understanding the process of immigrant adaptation and the significance of religion in the production and maintenance of ethnicity and identity in immigrant groups. My realization that there are multiple pathways by which assimilation can occur and that significant difference exists not only amongst immigrant ethnic groups but between immigrant generational stages as to how they experience the process of assimilation.

---

[1] Audi, John (1993). The place of religious arguments in a free and democratic society. *San Diego Law Review*, V.30, (4).

To summarize this study combines my interest in the cognitive processes that exist for justification of opinions expressed in the public sphere with the issue of immigrant adaptation to a new host environment. Like a camera obscura I plan to utilize the opinions expressed publically by immigrants on substantive issues of economic and social concerns to develop an understanding of immigrant adaptation and the changes that occur over time and within the process of assimilation.

At a manifest level this work is about the post1965 immigrant and the stances they take on substantive issues of social and economic concerns. It is also about religion, specifically religious orthodoxy and the relationship of beliefs, praxis, and the subjective opinion immigrants have about their own religious identity to their expressed attitudes on key social and economic issues.

At a more significant and interpretive level it is about capturing the changes which take place within the new immigrant population as the immigrant group transitions to mainstream American life. This study intends to use the data gathered from immigrant responders by the University of Chicago through their General Social Survey to measure differences in religious orthodoxy (religious intensity), authoritarianism and communitarianism, between immigrant generational stages to capture changes that occur within the process of adaptation for the new immigrant group.

In summary my goal for this work is simple: to provide an opportunity for readers to think a bit about immigrants and the complex processes of adaptation. To contemplate how the immigrant may differ from the American mainstream and how they are similar. If this work challenges what we believe we know for a fact about the new immigrants and what we believe to be true but is in reality based upon our biases, so much for the better. In the final analysis we are all immigrants and this in many ways is a study about all of us.

Significance of Study

This study will enrich our understanding of the changes or identity shifts that the immigrant experiences as part of the process of assimilation and accommodation as they transition from immigrant generation, to 1.5 generation, to second generation. It will augment our existing knowledge about the new immigrants and hopefully motivate other scholars to research their own questions about the post1965 immigrant population.

During the past 20 years researchers of religion, immigration, and ethnicity have studied how religion influences the lives of post 1965 immigrants in the United States. The majority of this research has been case studies of institutional religious practice focusing upon individual religious groups and organizations. According to Cadge and Eckland (2007)[2], the greatest strengths of this research are also its greatest weaknesses: a reliance on richly descriptive individual case studies and an absence of systematic analytic comparisons and synthesis of large data sets. Cage and Eklund believe that in the analysis of the relationship between religion and immigration, religion must be considered a powerful variable that influences immigrant economic mobility and civic and political participation. This study attempts to fill in the knowledge gaps that Cage and Eklund have identified by focusing on religious orthodoxy (religious intensity) and what has been theorized as its potentially causative relationship to the development of opinions on substantive issues of social and economic concern. The findings of this research study will lead the reader to broaden their view as to what acts as motivation and justification for opinion formation to include a multiplicity of sub-cultural identities as problem solving tool.

Formally the main objectives of this text are two- fold.

1. Through the process of a comparative analysis of the immigrant generational stages and a critical reflection upon the accompanying changes in expression of opinions on substantive issues of social and economic concerns I will add to our knowledge of the new immigrant groups and how their changes in opinion reflect changes in life values that occur as part of their adaptation to a new host environment.
2. The study will demonstrate the theoretical significance of a religious world view (religious orthodoxy) and intersecting subcultural identities as explanatory theories in the creation of life lenses; life lenses, being instrumental in creating direction and pathways for action in the real world. This study will answer the question whether religious orthodoxy (religious intensity) is the primary, most salient and consistent life lenses or moral compass for opinion formation across immigrant generational stages or only one of a multiplicity of salient subcultural identities that is accessed to justify action.

In this work I will use attitudes expressed in public on substantive issues of social and economic concerns to highlight significant changes

---

[2] Cadge, Wendy and Eckland, Elaine (2007). Immigration and religion, *Annual Rev. of Sociology*, 33:359-379.

along two separate continuums that will be interpreted as demonstrating changes in identity:

1. authoritarian – modernism (the extent to which opinions are formed based upon religious principles or individual choice).
2. Communitarianism – individualism (a sense of economic mutual support or individualism whereby the poor are responsible for their own fates).

At a secondary level, this work is also comparing two theoretical lenses, religious worldview or religious orthodoxy and multiple subcultural identities -intersectionality, to assess which has the greater explanatory power, in understanding immigrant identity changes.

To paraphrase Jurgen Habermas, all action is both symbolic and communicative. The task of this study is to interpret the symbolic and understand what is being communicated by immigrants in their adjustment to a new country. To successfully achieve this task, beliefs and practices must be situated within the context of culture and civil society. This study will analyze the complex relationship between religious orthodoxy (religious intensity), immigrant generational status and subcultural identities in the formation of opinions on key social and economic issues in order to capture immigrant identity changes. It will utilize two anchoring points to accomplish this task; i.e., immigration and secondly, the role of religious orthodoxy and sub-cultural identities in value transmission. It is my contention that by doing so, beliefs and practices, as measured by opinions, will be placed in an interpretive context.

This text will add to the existing knowledge about the post1965 immigrant groups by addressing several essential questions. 1) How does religious expression in the public sphere co-relate to sub cultural identities? 2) In combination with each other, how do they create expressed opinions within new immigrant groups? 3) Is there variability between immigrant generational stages for expressed opinions and if so what explains this variability? 4). How does immigrant generational stage influence the relationship between religious orthodoxy, sub-cultural identities and opinion formation? A recent study (Davis and Robinson1996b:758)[3] has addressed the significance of religious identity and the intersection of social class and race as independent variables in opinion formation. However unlike this work, the study did not focus upon new immigrant groups as a part of their study sample.

---

[3] Davis,Nancy and Robinson, Robert (1996b). Are the rumors of war exaggerated? *American Journal of Sociology*, 102(3):756-787.

At this point I will comment briefly upon the conceptual differences between personality and identity, the explanatory theories associated with each and how these constructs relate to this study. I will then close with a few salient comments taken from the works of Pierre Bourdieu that I believe are admonitions worth contemplating.

According to the Diagnostic and Statistical Manual for Mental Health (2000:826)[4], personality is *"an enduring pattern or patterns of perceiving, relating to and thinking about the environment and oneself"*. Personality makes the individual unique, arises from within and remains fairly constant throughout one's life. There are numerous theoretical explanations for the development of one's personality ranging from classical Freudian theory to the behaviorism of John Watson (Mitchell and Black 1995).[5] A more in-depth discussion of personality is beyond the scope of this book and not germane to the focus of this work.

I take identity to be a broader and more fluid construct than personality. Identity is a collection of aspects or a set of characteristics by which a person is known or is recognized as a member of a group (Webster Collegiate 2003).[6] Identity is often used as a category of human experience (Wren 2002).[7] It can be thought of as cultural identity forged in a social and political context. Identities are narratives fashioned in discourse and located within specific historical or institutional sites with specific discourse functions and practices (Hall 1996).[8] Simply put, personality is consistent, located within the individual and gives greater acknowledgment to psychological factors. Identity is fluid and located within a cultural- historical context and gives greater acknowledgment to sociological and collective factors. It is changes of identity that will be the focus of our attention. I will revisit the issue of identity and its relationship to the theory of sub-cultural identity later in the study.

I will address in detail in the following literature review, the two explanatory lenses that I will use to gage changes between immigrant generational stages. However, for the moment in keeping with setting the frame of this work, I will present them briefly.

The first, the theory of moral cosmology posits that the creation of a religious worldview, based upon an individual's religious orthodoxy or religious intensity, leads to specific attitude formation in the life world.

---

[4] DSM-IV-TR (2000). *American Psychiatric Association,* p. 826.
[5] Mitchell, Stephen and Black, Margret (1995). *Freud and beyond,* Basic Books.
[6] *Webster's Dictionary,* eleventh edition, Collegiate, 2003.
[7] Wren,Thomas (2002). *Cultural identity and personal identity.* In Personal and Moral Identity, Edited by A.W.Musschunga, Springer.
[8] Hall, Stewart (1996). *Who needs identity.* London Publications.

This is so irrespective of the individual's self -identified religious tradition. In a true Weberian sense looking to ideas as the explanation for action. Traditional literature on religion and subcultural identity development has been based primarily on studies of Christian immigrant groups at the turn of the 20th century. These studies emphasized religious rituals, especially those practiced in congregations, as the major mechanism for preserving ethnic culture and identity (Min 2010).[9] Davis and Robinson (2006)[10], as well as Starks and Robinson (2009)[11], broaden the above traditional focus by connecting the religious world view, as expressed through cultural beliefs and practices to issues of social and economic justice through an analysis of moral cosmology. The theory of Moral Cosmology explains the formation and justification of political opinion by an individual's adherence to religious orthodoxy or modernism; that is their religious beliefs, belongings, and behaviors. It posits that the religiously orthodox are theological communitarian in perceiving individuals as belonging to a larger community of believers and subject to god's law and greater plan. The religiously orthodox, irrespective of religious tradition, are disposed towards economic communitarianism whereby the state should provide for the poor, reduce inequality, and meet society's needs through economic interventions. Modernists are theologically individualistic in seeing individuals as having to make moral decisions in a temporal context and as responsible for their own destinies. Modernists are inclined to economic individualism whereby the poor are responsible for their own fates. In the domain of cultural issues the religiously orthodox are found to be more conservative than the modernists and inclined to take an authoritarian position on socio-cultural issues; one which enforces what they believe to be gods divinely mandated stand on moral issues.

The second, the theory of multiple sub-cultural identities, focuses upon identity (collective) rather than a religious worldview in its attempt to explain attitude formation. It recognizes the salience of identity roles and their stability across time and situations but acknowledges that the salience of a given role can diminish and be superseded by another role more significant for the individual (collective) at that given moment in time. It

---

[9] Min, Pyong Gap (2010). *Preserving ethnicity through religion in America*, pp1-2, New York University Press.
[10] Davis,Nancy and Robinson, Robert (2006).The egalitarian face of the Islamic Orthodoxy, *American Sociological Review*, V. 71.
[11] Starks,Brian and Robinson, Robert (2009). Two approaches to religion and politics: Moral Cosmology and Sub-cultural Identity. *Journal for the Scientific Study of Religion*, V. 48, no.4.

views society as: *"a mosaic of relatively durable patterned interactions and relationships, differentiated yet organized, embedded in an array of groups, organizations, communities and institutions, and intersected by crosscutting boundaries of class, ethnicity, age, gender, religion, and other variables"*. It is these salient sub-cultural identities that motivates and justifies individual and collective action. (Stryker and Burke 2000:285).[12]

The multiple sub-cultural identity model has its origins in seeing religious movements among Protestants as creating identity spaces (world view) from which they define themselves relative to other groups (Stark and Robinson 2009).[13] The sub- cultural identities approach is an alternative- theoretical reply to Berger (1967)[14] who conceptualized religion as a "sacred canopy" under which religious believers developed their own unique systems of meaning. Berger hypothesized that with the spread of secularization as a consequence of modern pluralism, there would develop an erosion of the viability of a single sacred canopy. Smith et al., (1997)[15] replies, that the development of communities of meaning has been altered with the spread of modern pluralism but that the outcome is not simply secularization. Instead as the society- wide sacred canopy of belief (world view) disintegrates, smaller communities will create their own sacred umbrellas under which their believers will develop their own systems of belief. This will lead to the establishment of religious sub-cultural identities which allowed adherents to develop identity spaces which are unique and associated with their own vocabulary, expectations, and systems of symbolic meaning. I am broadening Smith's position in that I believe that the construct of sub-cultural identity is not exclusive to religious traditions but extends to other communities of meaning (symbolic) which I hypothesize are relevant to opinion formation. Communities whose boundaries are defined by gender, ethnicity, social class and immigrant generation.

---

[12] Stryker, Sheldon and Burke, Peter (2000). The past, present and future of an identity theory. *Social Psychology Quarterly*, vol.63, No. 4, pp. 284-297.

[13] Stark,Brian and Robinson, Robert (2009). Two approaches to religion and politics: Moral Cosmology and Sub-cultural Identity, *Journal For the Scientific Study of Religion*, v. 48, no. 4, pp. 65-669, December.

[14] Berger, Peter (1967). *The sacred canopy: Elements of a sociological theory of religion*. Doubleday.

[15] Smith, Emerson, Gallagher, Kennedy and Sikkirk (1997). The myth of cultural wars: *In Cultural Wars in American Politics*, edited by Williams, pp. 175-195, Aldine de Gruyter.

I believe that unlike the structuralists that Bourdieu critiqued (1994:4-5)[16], I am not "*creating a grand theory without agents in a reaction against existentialism*". For as Bourdieu admonishes, social agents (people): "*are not automata regulated like clocks, acting in accordance with laws which they do not understand*". In this light the study takes the position that a religious world view or one's religious orthodoxy is not sufficient to explain opinion formation in the public sphere. In reality a multiplicity of subcultural identities exist as salient forces in opinion formation.

Overall Research Design

Data from the General Social Survey conducted by the National Opinion Research Center of the University of Chicago was used for this study; specifically waves 2006, 2008 and 2010. The GSS was the most suitable data survey for our purposes as it included questions which allowed for the measurement of religious orthodoxy/modernism, identify respondent's religious tradition, gender, and contained questions addressing key economic and social issues. It also allowed analysis across the three target groups that we wished to study (immigrant generation, 1.5 generation, second-generation). The total number of respondents by group was as follows: immigrants (604), 1.5 generation (209), 2.0 generation (271) and multiple generation reference (5483). Please see Appendix E.1 for the demographic profile by main groups.

Measurement and Data Collection

Independent Variables: There are three independent variables in this research study that are the focus of attention: 1. immigrant generational stage, 2. religious traditions (Protestant and Catholic), 3. gender.

In addition there are three dependent variables; 1. religious orthodoxy, 2. economic communitarianism/individualism and 3. social authoritarianism/ modernism.

The first independent variable was immigrant generational stage. Respondents were assigned as follows: first generation immigrant stage, respondents not born in the United States; the 1.5 generation consisted of respondents who were not born in the United States but who immigrated to the United States before the age of 16. The second immigrant generational stage was comprised of respondents who were born in this

---

[16] Bourdieu, Pierre (1994)., *In other words*, Polity Press, Cambridge, pp4-5; p.9.

country but whose parents were immigrants. The reference group functioned as a comparison or control group. In order to be a respondent assigned to the reference group, the respondent and both parents needed to be born in the United States, thus making the reference group the third immigrant generation.

The second independent variable was religious tradition. Religious tradition was based upon respondent's self-selection. In this study in order to obtain healthy cell size for analysis, we were able to analyze data from only Protestants and Roman Catholics respondents. Again for statistical reason we were not able to separate protestant responders into denominations or separate them into evangelical and mainline traditions. Roman Catholics respondents were also aggregated for healthy cell size. Analysis was conducted both across religious traditions and within religious tradition and between immigrant generational stages.

The third independent variable was gender of the respondent. Analysis was conducted both across gender and within gender between immigrant generational stages.

Dependent Variables: The first dependent variable was religious orthodoxy or intensity of religiosity. Religious orthodoxy was measured by using a 12 item weighted scale comprised of three core dimensions: biblical literalism, practice and subjective religiosity. Similar to Davis and Robinson (2006)[17] I prefer a measure that classifies individuals based upon their beliefs and practice rather than relying solely on a self- assessment scale. Again following the path set by Davis and Robinson, I use the labels modernist and orthodoxy to avoid potential political connotations often associated with the terms progressive and conservative. All twelve questions were asked in all three of the GSS data waves. See appendix A for the questions comprising the indices of religious orthodoxy.

The second and third dependent variables were issues of economic and social concerns. There were 10 weighted items that comprise the indices of social and economic issues. Seven items comprise the indices assessing social issues and three items comprise the indices assessing economic issues. All 10 questions were asked in each of the three GSS data waves. Please see appendix B for the questions that comprise the indices of social and economic issues.

Data Analysis and Interpretation: This study measures how different generations of recent immigrants to the U.S. (post1965) vary in their religious orthodoxy (intensity of religiosity) and in their stances on social and economic issues. This is an in- direct observational study based upon self-reported data. I rely upon three different waves (2006, 2008, and

---

[17] Davis, Nancy and Robinson, Robert, ibid.

2010) of the General Social Survey (GSS) conducted by the University of Chicago for the respondent pool. Multiple waves are necessary in order to assure ample sample sizes. To gauge religious orthodoxy or the intensity of religiosity and differences in attitudes for economic and social issues, indices are used (3). Indices are re-expressions made by combining the specific questions addressing each of our three dependent variables. The re-expressions for each indices are interval or scale data. The higher scores equate to a higher religiosity or religious orthodoxy, and a greater sense of individualism and authoritativeness on economic and social issues. See appendix C.1, C.2 and C.3 for dependent variable indices.

The first stage of data analysis utilized the indices of religious orthodoxy to measure and compare religious orthodoxy between all groups; capturing changes/shifts in beliefs, practice and subjective religiosity for the immigrant generational stage, 1.5 generation and second generation.

The analysis of variance (ANOVA) methodology was employed to discern the levels of religious orthodoxy (intensity of religiosity) between the four main groups (Immigrant, 1.5 generation, Second generation and Reference). The One-way ANOVA determines the main effects of the groups. The main groups are nominal data. The strength of ANOVA is that in addition to denoting significant statistical difference it allows for statistical comparison between groups.

The text also studied the intersection of specific reference groups or subcultural identities for their interaction with the main groups. By overlaying these interactions with the four groups, immigrant generational stage, 1.5 generation, second generation and reference group (each group has one level of analysis and each intersect has two levels; Gender-Male and Female; Religious Tradition-Catholic and Protestant) a two-way cross design was created to assess this intersection.

To prevent a Type I error (find a significant difference where there is none) in the Two-way ANOVA, post hoc-tests were utilized. In the analysis of intersection of gender and immigrant generational stage I selected the 'least significant difference' method (LSD) as being the most liberal and statistically powerful of the post hoc tests. In the analysis of the intersection of religious tradition and immigrant generational stages (which did not attain normality with the index data), I selected the 'Scheffe' post hoc test as it is a conservative analytic tool that effectively controls for the overall error rate.

Formulation and Hypothesis

Through the review of the literature I will have demonstrated that religion matters and is significant to the immigrant in their adaptation to a new host environment. I will have demonstrated that religion is a salient subcultural identity but not the only subcultural identity in the motivation and justification of opinion formation on a wide range of social and economic issues. I will show that the adaptation process for the immigrant necessitates change; the immigrant is not the same at the time of his/her migration as when they are fully integrated into mainstream society. The questions before the contemporary researcher of immigration are important and numerous. What are the changes taking place within the immigrant population as part of their adaptation to the new host society and what are the variables that are influencing these changes? Does the immigrant become more individualistic and modernistic through the process of adaptation and integration? What are the variables that are driving these changes? Is religious orthodoxy or a multiplicity of subcultural identities most significant for the immigrant in the change process and their opinion formation on substantive issues? What is the effect of intersection of other subcultural identities with religion on opinions addressing important contemporary concerns? Can we observe patterns within these changes that will lead to viable predictions?

The following hypotheses are framed by my belief that immigrants begin as traditionalists and develop into modernists in their positions addressing both social and economic issues. They become less communitarian on economic issues and less religiously orthodox as part of the process of acculturation and assimilation. In effect, over multiple generations, their identity shifts to mirror the identity of the mainstream population.

Specifically for this research study, I predict that significant variability will be found to exist between the immigrant generational stage and the other target groups (1.5 generation, 2.0 generation) as well as between the immigrant generational stage and the reference group for all three of our dependent variables; religious orthodoxy, social concerns, economic concerns. However the variability will not follow patterns predicted by the theoretical paradigm of religious worldview or the theory Moral Cosmology. In point, the theoretical view of multiple subcultural identities and intersectionality will be of greater benefit to our understanding of the immigrant adaption process.

Based upon the literature review I have crafted my hypothesis in a traditional theoretical direction, expressing the significance of a religious world view or religious orthodoxy in the justification and motivation for opinion formation. As the reader will see, these hypotheses were not supported. I have left them crafted in this direction so that their rejection makes a stronger case for the need to develop a wider and less hegemonic perspective for opinion formation in the public sphere.

Hypothesis 1: *The immigrant generational stage will be more religiously orthodox than the reference group and all other target group.* Research demonstrates that religion is both an anchor for new immigrants and a means of maintaining ethnic identity. The immigrant generational stage's religious worldview (religious orthodoxy) will lead them to be more literal in their biblical interpretation, more active in their religious practice, and to experience a greater sense of religiosity than all other target groups and reference group.

Hypothesis 2: *The immigrant generational stage will be more communitarian on economic issues and more authoritarian on social issues (looking towards religious doctrine to define economic and acceptable social behavior) then any other target group or the reference group.*

Hypothesis 3: *A religious worldview or religious orthodoxy, as expressed by the theory of Moral Cosmology is viable and the most salient explanatory theory in predicting the stances on economic and social issues for the post 1965 immigrant population.*

Hypotheses 4: *Significant variability will be found across religious traditions (Protestant and Catholic), for the dependent variables, religious orthodoxy and social and economic issues. However, the variability on social and economic issues will be correlated to degree of religious orthodoxy (religious intensity) and not correlated to a religious tradition (Catholic/Protestant).*

Hypothesis 5: *Significant variability will be found across gender for the dependent variables, religious orthodoxy and social and economic issues. However, variability on social and economic issues will be correlated to degree of religious orthodoxy (religious intensity) and not correlated to gender.*

Organization of Text

The literature review consists of four chapters (chapters 2, 3, 4, and 5) each presenting part of the frame for this text. Chapter 2 addresses the changing face of immigration in the United States by presenting a brief demographic overview of the post1965 immigrant population and a comparison of the post1965 immigrant flow to previous periods of immigration. Chapter 2 concludes with a review of the theoretical changes which have occurred in immigration theory. Chapter 3 presents an overview of the significance of religious practices and institutional religion to immigration. Chapter 4 introduces the relationship between religion and politics in the United States and makes the case for culture as a bridge between the two. The literature review concludes with chapter 5 which presents the theoretical frames of moral cosmology (religious world view) and subcultural identity and intersectionality.

The results section is presented in three separate but related chapters (chapter 6, 7 and 8). Chapter 6 presents data for the comparison between immigrant generational stages for the effect of religious orthodoxy upon economic and social issues. Chapter 7 adds the variable of religious traditions and presents the data analyzing the comparisons between religious traditions (Catholic/Protestant) for the combined effect of religious orthodoxy and immigrant generational stages upon economic and social issues. Chapter 8 introduces gender as a variable and presents the analysis of the comparison between gender for the combined effect of religious orthodoxy and immigrant generational stages upon economic and social issues. The work concludes with the discussion of the data (chapter 9) and summary remarks in (chapter 10). I have provided the list of GSS questions used to construct the indices of religious orthodoxy and economic and social concerns in appendices A and B. The indices scores are located in appendices C.1, C.2 and C.3. Pearson Rho correlations can be found in appendices D.1, D.2 and D.3. Finally demographic profiles are to be found in appendices E.1, E.2, and E.3.

CHAPTER TWO

THE CHANGING FACE OF IMMIGRATION IN AMERICA

Chapter Overview

I begin chapter 2 by setting the frame for our conversation of immigration and religion by providing a demographic perspective of the post1965 immigrant flow. Where did they originate? What do we know about them socio-economically? What religions do they identify with? These questions are essential to our descriptive frame. I will then present the major theoretical issues concerning immigrant adaptation to the new host country by focusing upon the integrated processes of acculturation and assimilation.

Section 1:
Demographic Overview of the Post 1965 Immigrant Flow

Historically there have been three major immigrant flows to the United States in the last 150 years (Alba and Nee 2000)[1]. The first between 1840 and 1880 was comprised of immigrants from the United Kingdom, Germany and Ireland. The high point of this immigration flow was at the end of this period of immigration when slightly less than 800,000 immigrants came to our shores. Some 96.5% of these immigrants were from Northwestern Europe, slightly under 5% from southeastern Europe. The second immigrant wave occurred between 1891 and 1930 and was comprised primarily of Italian, Russian, Hungarian, Polish and southern and eastern European immigrants. The high point of this immigrant flow was 1905 when slightly over 1.2 million immigrants arrived during that year. Some 46% of these immigrants were from Northwestern Europe, 45% from southeastern Europe, 6% from Latin America and the Caribbean and just under 3% from Asia and the Middle East. The post1965 immigrants had a high point of immigration in 1990 when over 1.8 million

---

[1] Alba and Nee, ibid, p. 170, table 5.1, legal immigration to the United States, 1820 through 2000.

immigrants arrived. Demographically the population was quite different from the preceding immigrant flows. 6.5% of the immigrants were from North Western Europe, 8.5% were from southeastern Europe, 45% were from Latin America and the Caribbean and some 35% from Asia and the Middle East (Min 2002).[2]

A large share of the demographic diversification is attributable to the Immigration Act of 1965. This act abolished the discriminatory 1920's era country -of – origin quotas and substituted occupational preference and family reunification provisions through which legislators hoped for an infusion of skilled workers into the US economy and an end to the separation of families which had been a bye product of previous immigration policy. What we now recognize to be among the main effects of the law, the brain drain of professionals from Asia and the multiplier effect, the subsequent reunification of their families in the United States, was largely unanticipated (Warner 2000).[3]

In addition the legalization of some 2.7 million former undocumented immigrants in special agricultural workers under the amnesty provision of the 1986 immigration reform and control contributed to their record. According to the 2010 census data, there are some 40 million foreign-born legal residents in the United States. 55% of these or approximately 21million originate in Latin America or the Caribbean. An additional one third roughly 13million are from Central America with Mexico comprising some 25% (3 million) of this group. Asia comprises an additional 15% or 6 million of the current legal resident population.

Recent estimates suggest that approximately 23% of the American population is an immigrant or the child of an immigrant; 1.5 and second generation (Alba and Nee 2003).[4] Based on data presented in the first wave of the New Immigrant Survey, a nationally representative survey of post 1965 legal immigrants to the United States, the new immigrants are increasing the racial and ethnic diversity of America, as well as bringing larger numbers of adherents of non-Christian religions to the United States (National Immigration Survey, Princeton University).[5]

---

[2] Min, Pyong Gap, (2002). Mass migration to the United States, p.4, table 1.1, immigration to the United States by decade region and race 1841 through 1996, Altamira Press.
[3] Warner, Stephan, (2000). Religion and the new immigrants, *American Studies*, 41:pp. 267-286.
[4] Alba, Richard, and Nee, Victor (2003). *Remaking the American mainstream: Assimilation and contemporary immigration.* Cambridge, Massachusetts, Harvard University press.
[5] http://nis.princeton.edu

Jasso et al., (2003)[6] studied the religious preferences among new immigrants aged 18 or over at time of admission to permanent residence. Some two thirds 64.7% expressed a preference for a Christian religion. Not surprisingly, given the high percentage of immigrants from Mexico, Latin America and the Philippines, the largest preference expressed was for Catholicism 42%. The proportions reporting a preference for orthodox or Protestant religions were 4.2% and 18.6% respectively. 8% of immigrants identified as Muslim.

Again citing Jasso et al., the religious preferences among recent immigrants is significantly different from the native born population in the United States. The proportion of native born residents that identify as Christian is 85% significantly larger than the 65% for the immigrant group. Secondly the proportion of Catholics is almost twice as large among the immigrants as among native born; 42% versus 22%. The proportion reporting religion outside the classical Judeo-Christian tradition is more than four times greater among recent immigrants than among native born; 16.7% versus 4%.

Jasso et al. also analyzed the average years of schooling completed among recent immigrants 25 and over by religious preference. Among men, years of education ranged from 12.1 years (Catholics) to a high of 16.4 years (Buddhists). Among women, this span was from 10.8 for Muslims to 15.4 for Hindus. According to Jasso educational differential across religious preference groups is more than four years among men (approximately the difference between high school and college graduation). Among women the years of education differential is slightly larger, 4.6 years. The most educated immigrants are among men, Buddhists and Muslims 16.4 and15.1 average years respectively. Among women the most educated are Hindus and Orthodox Christians, which averaged 15.4 and 15 years respectively. Those immigrants with the lowest years of education were Catholic men 12.1 years, followed closely by Hindus 12.2 years. On average Jewish immigrants obtained 13.1 years of schooling for men. Among women those with the least years of education were Muslims (10.8) years followed by Catholic (11.4) years and Protestants (12.1) years.

Zhou (2003)[7] tells us that there are five major distinctive features between previous immigrant flows and contemporary immigration. The first addresses the issue of absorption rates. Despite the similarity in the

---

[6] Jasso et al., (2003). In Haddad et al., eds. *Religion and immigration*, Alta Mira Press, pp. 220-221.
[7] Zhou, Min,(2002). The changing face of America: Immigration, race, ethnicity and social mobility. Chapter two, in *Mass Migration to the United States*, ibid.

absolute numbers the rate of contemporary immigration relative to the total US population is much lower than that of earlier immigration flows. The US population has more than tripled during the course of the 20th century. The comparatively low rate of contemporary immigration implies a more modest overall impact on the US population today than in the past. This impact is disproportionately localized in areas of high immigration not only in the historic gateway cities but also in smaller urban or suburban areas in which few immigrants had settled in the past

The second distinctive feature addresses the rate of immigrant return to sending country. Contemporary immigration rates are considerably lower today than in the past. It was estimated that for every 100 immigrants during the past decades of high immigration (previous two major immigrant flows), 36 had returned to their homelands. In contrast between 1971 and 1990, less than a quarter had returned. This trend indicates a steadier growth for post 1965 immigrants than for previous immigrant groups; demonstrating also that contemporary immigrants are more likely than earlier immigrants to remain in the United States.

The third feature is that unlike immigration in the past contemporary immigration is accompanied by a much larger number of undocumented immigrants. This event has partially been created by our reliance on Mexican immigration for cheap agriculture labor, as well as the operation of migrant networks that assist undocumented immigration entering and staying in the United States (Massey 1995). [8]

The fourth compared to immigration in the past, today's inflows consist of immigrants of color, which are much more visible. The newcomers are predominantly from non-European countries. Since 1980 more than 85% of the immigrants admitted to the United States come from Asia and the Americas and only 10% from Europe compared to more than 90% of the earlier peak. In particular, the share of immigrants from the Americas as a proportion of total legal immigrant admissions has risen substantially from 25% of the 1950 moving to 39% in the 1960s and jumping up to 50% since the 1980s. Similarly the share of immigrants from Asia as a proportion of the total admissions grew from a tiny 5% in the 1950s, to 11% in the 1960s and 33% in the 70s and stayed at roughly 35% since 1980.

The fifth distinctive feature of post 1965 immigration is the all-time high of non-immigrants arriving in the states temporarily as tourists, students, temporary workers and traders or investors. This group of non-immigrants contains a significant pool of potential immigrants. In

---

[8] Massey, Douglas.(1995). The new immigration and ethnicity in the United States, *Population and Development Review*, 21 (3): 631-652.

summation a lower rate of emigration, greater numbers of undocumented immigrants and refugees and an increasing pool of potential immigrants among non-immigrants add to the complexity of contemporary immigration. In 1995 almost half of the legal immigrants admitted to the United States had their non-immigrant visas adjusted to remain in the United States. Approximately 40% of the total number of undocumented immigrants is comprised by immigrants who overstayed their legal time in country (Zhou).

Spatially, the turn-of-the-century immigrants were highly concentrated along the northeastern seaboard and in the Midwest. For them the top five most preferred state destinations were New York, Pennsylvania, Illinois, Massachusetts and New Jersey. In contrast today's newcomers are highly concentrated not only in states or urban areas traditionally attracting most immigrants but also in states or urban areas that had few immigrants in the past. Since 1971, the top five states of immigrant intended residence have been California, New York, Florida, Texas and New Jersey accounting for almost 2 out of every three newly admitted immigrants (Zhou 2003).[9]

Finally, the new immigrants differ significantly from the turn-of-the-century immigrant population as well as amongst themselves in the range of variability of their social and economic capital. The image of a poor uneducated and unskilled immigrant is not generalizable to the entire post1965 immigrant flow.

Section 2:
The Changing Theory of Immigration:
Theoretical Perspectives upon the Dual and Integrated
Processes of Acculturation and Assimilation

This section through a historical presentation of the theoretical perspectives of the processes of immigrant adaptation captures both the shifting social view towards the process of immigrant adaptation and the increased awareness of the complexity of immigrant adaptation to the host environment. I present this section to expand our awareness of the breadth of the immigrant assimilation processes and to emphasize the life- world demands that are embedded within this process. This theoretical section posits that the change in the majoritarian perspective of immigration and the shift towards a multi-trajectory and context bound conceptual frame is indicative of societal acceptance of diversity and social construction as a viable way of knowing. It is my contention that by presenting both the

---

[9] Zhou, Min, ibid, pp. 69.

sociological, psychological and economic variables that we believe comprises the construct of assimilation and the life-world demands that an immigrant must face, we will more clearly frame the immigrant change process which is after all the focus of this study.

The immigrant journey from immigrant generational stage, to 1.5 generation, to 2.0 generation to mainstream American life requires in my opinion, significant and multiple changes in their identification to salient reference groups. I will return to this hypothesized relationship between reference group identification or subcultural identities in chapters four and five of this literature review. For now, I will present a brief theoretical overview of the processes of assimilation and what we understand it to entail in the post -modern U.S.

Assimilation in our contemporary society is a contentious construct. Since the 1960s it has been cast in a negative light; as an ethnocentric and patronizing position on minority peoples struggling to retain and express their cultural and ethnic identity. Nathan Glazer (1993)[10] in his article: "Is Assimilation Dead?" makes the point that the term Americanization may be acceptable but not so for assimilation. Frantz Fanon (1988)[11] views the process of acculturation and assimilation as the enterprise of de-acculturation. A larger project constructed by the majoritarian culture that encompasses both economic and biological enslavement. Fanon cautions that unilaterally created normative value of a specific culture deserves our critical reflection. Fanon (1988:305)[12]; *"There is first affirmed the existence of human groups having no culture; then of a hierarchy of cultures; and finally the concept of cultural relativity."*

Alba and Nee (2003:1)[13] in a likeminded fashion proclaim that the assimilation concept of an earlier era is: *"now condemned for the expectation that minority groups would inevitably want to shed their own cultures as if these were old skins no longer possessing any vital force and wrap themselves in the mantle of Anglo American culture."*

The questions before today's researcher interested in immigration and its accompanying processes are complex. What does the process of assimilation look like in our postmodern, culturally and ethnically diverse society? Is the paradigm of acculturation and assimilation still a viable

---

[10] Glazer, Nathan, (1993). Is assimilation dead? *Annals* 530, November, 123.

[11] Fannon, Frantz (1988). *Towards the African revolution. Monthly Review Press,* 305-311.

[12] Fannon, ibid.

[13] Alba, Richard, and Nee, Victor (2003). *Remaking the American mainstream: Assimilation and contemporary immigration.* Cambridge, Massachusetts, Harvard University Press, p.1.

theoretical concept that has explanatory power to bring into focus the experiences of the contemporary immigrant? How do we build upon existing knowledge on immigrant adaptation to shed light on the immigrant adaptive process in the current context?

Historically, assimilation as a theoretical paradigm for understanding immigration is traceable to the Chicago School of Sociology. In the early 20th century, Robert Park (1930)[14] tasked himself with the challenge of understanding the experiences of immigrants who were migrating to the mid-west and Chicago in particular. Park possibly provided the earliest definition of assimilation: *"a process of interpenetration and fusion in which persons and groups acquire the memories, sentiments and attitudes of other persons and groups and by sharing their experience and history are incorporated with them in a common cultural life."*(Park1930:281).[15] Analyzed closely it becomes evident that the major interpretive misunderstanding of Park's work, that assimilation requires the erasure of all signs of ethnic origins is not valid. Park did understand assimilation as the process that changes the immigrant and that is essential if ethnic minorities are to become integrated into the mainstream of American civil society. However, he perceived it to be a fusion of cultures. A theoretical view that was I believe, consciously overlooked by American mainstream society in a search for solidarity or in a Fanonesque fashion, with the intent towards creating social stratification and majoritarian group domination.

The mid- 20th century was the high point of the "melting pot" metaphor for assimilation. This construct was integral to the American self- understanding and the center point of sociological investigations of race and ethnicity. Milton Gordon (1964)[16] in his instrumental text: *"Assimilation in American Life''* deconstructed the threads associated with the processes of acculturation and assimilation. Gordon was perhaps the first to view the immigrant's assimilation process as a multidimensional construct. For Gordon, acculturation or cultural assimilation (Gordon used both terms somewhat interchangeable), was the dimension of immigrant adaptation that came first and was inevitable. He defined acculturation as the minority group's adoption of the cultural patterns of the host society. These patterns extended beyond the acquisition of language and dress (observable) and included cognitive constructs representing the individual's inner or psychological self. Emotional expressions, core

---

[14] Park, Robert (1930). Assimilation; In Seligman and Johnson, eds., *Encyclopedia of the Social Sciences*, Macmillan, p. 281.
[15] Park, ibid.
[16] Gordon, Milton (1964). *Assimilation in American life*. Oxford University Press.

values of life and an individual's life goals were considered as essential components in the acculturation process. Gordon unlike Park stressed a one way process of acculturation except in the area of religion. Here the immigrant group was able to maintain their core religious culture unchanged by the acculturation process.

Interestingly, Gordon posited that acculturation can occur in the absence of assimilation and that this stage of "acculturation only" could last indefinitely. Gordon (1964:72)[17]: *"cultural assimilation or acculturation is likely to be the first of the types of assimilation to occur when a minority group arrives on the scene; cultural assimilation or acculturation of a minority group may take place even when none of the other types of assimilation occurs simultaneous or later, and this condition of "acculturation only" may continue indefinitely.* This thread was continued by later researchers who acknowledged the immigrant's need to maintain and transmit ethnicity despite pressures to assimilate.

Gordon's major theoretical hypothesis was that of structural assimilation; the process through which the immigrant group is integrated and accepted into the primary or host society. Gordon believed that there were several sub types or categories of assimilation; cultural, structural, marital, identity, prejudice, discrimination, and civic. For Gordon once structural assimilation occurred, all other types of assimilation would follow.

Alba and Nee reflecting upon Gordon's work, make a valid observation that the integrated processes of assimilation and acculturation are not a one-way process; occurring not just through changes in one group that make it more like another but through changes in two or more groups that shrink the differences between them. In short acculturation is a process of group convergence or bilateral conversion. Acculturation is not limited to the substitution of one cultural element for its equivalent whether the replacement comes from majority or minority cultures. In the process of bilateral convergence, the impact of minority ethnic cultures on the mainstream culture creates an expansion of the range of what is considered normal behavior within the mainstream culture. This was a new insight; the recognition of the (subtle) blending of cultural expressiveness in every -day life, creating a multicultural context. According to Alba and Nee (2003:25)[18]:*"the cultural fusion that results, especially evident in urban life, makes the repertoire of styles, cuisine, popular culture, and myths an incremental process. One in which they become incorporated into American daily life."*

---

[17] Gordon, Milton, p.72, ibid.
[18] Alba and Nee, p.25, ibid.

In our modern world we barely recognize the examples of cultural fusion which surround us in daily life; hip-hop, rap music and Asian fusion cuisine readily come to mind. Orum (2005)[19] expands on this concept of cultural fusion. The contemporary immigrant community is a transnational community that possesses a life of its own and is capable of individual and collective action which directly and indirectly affects the mainstream or majoritarian culture.

The next major conceptual development in the reconstruction of the processes of acculturation and assimilation was a drifting away from the structural assimilation model and its hypothesized sequelae; the integration of immigrants into primary groups and their intermarriage with primary group partners as markers of successfully completing the assimilation process. Structural assimilation was replaced by theories focusing upon socio-economic assimilation. This theoretical shift was brought about by the post1965 immigrant bringing significant educational credentials, professional training and other forms of human capital to the table. It required a more sophisticated conceptualization of adaptation, where the contemporary immigrant was no longer viewed as starting at the bottom of the labor market. Socio- economic assimilation became the center piece for studying immigrant adaptation and was defined as the minority's participation in mainstream socio-economic institutions (labor market and education) on parity with other groups. Once fully assimilated it was thought that members of the immigrant minority would have the same life chances in the pursuit of contested goods and desirable occupations, as any other group. In theory, ethnic distinction and racial bias would lose their significance.

The next theoretical development can be attributed to Portes (1995)[20] and Portes and Zhou (1993)[21] and their conceptualization of multiple trajectories of adaptation in their work with second generation immigrants. This led to the theoretical formulation of segmented assimilation. Traditional theories of immigrant adaptation were linear and assumed a single trajectory whereby successive generations would make gradual progress towards integration into mainstream society. According to Min

---

[19] Orum, Anthony (2005). Circles of influence; Chains of command, *Social Forces*, 84 (2), pp.921-939.

[20] Portes, Alejandro (1995)."Segmented assimilation amongst new immigrant youth". *California's Immigrant Children*, Rumbaut and Cornelius, eds., University of California at San Diego.

[21] Portes, Alejandro and Zhou, In Min (1993). "The New second generation." *Annals of American Academy of Political and Social Sciences*, 530: 74-98.

(2002)[22] in the theory of segmented assimilation, descendants of the new immigrants can choose one of three different modes of adaptation depending on such variables as their race, their parent's socioeconomic status, residential locale and family/community structure. They can: 1) incorporate into the white middle class with a high level of social mobility through education; 2) incorporate into the minority youth culture with no opportunity for social mobility or; 3) demonstrate retention of ethnic culture with social mobility found within the ethnic community. By projecting three different modes of adaptation for different groups of immigrants, the theory of segmented assimilation rejects the one-way path of the classical assimilation. It introduced variability in adaptation but more significantly multiple end points in the adaptive process.

Continuing with the theme of multiple adaptation trajectories but within specific immigrant groups, Hurh and Kim (1984:74)[23] present their theoretical construct "adhesive assimilation", as a frame for understanding assimilation in the Korean immigrant community. According to Hurh and Kim, Korean adhesive assimilation is a variant of segmented ethnic assimilation.

Classical assimilation theory (Gordon) suggested that acculturation or cultural assimilation is a necessary but not a sufficient condition for structural assimilation to occur. Even the high socio- economic status of the Korean immigrant community may not lead to social assimilation. Hurh and Kim suggest that the Korean immigrant is structurally separated from the larger society regardless of their acculturation, socioeconomic status and length of stay in the United States. The Korean immigrant's perception of such structural limitation, limits their aspirations for social acceptance by the dominant group. As a defense against such limitations, Korean immigrants maintain and enhance their Korean ethnic attachment, in order to sustain their sense of security, primary group satisfaction, social recognition, and identity. In this specific case, the Korean immigrant's strong and persistent ethnic attachment may be an adaptive reaction to the ethnic and racial segregation inherent in the American social structure. As a response, the Korean immigrant's adaptation would be "adhesive"; that is they would be Americanized both culturally and socially but to a limited extent especially in the social dimension. Americanization would not replace or weaken any significant aspect of Korean traditional culture and social networks

---

[22] Min, Pyong Gap, (2002). Mass migration to the United States, Altamira Press.
[23] Hurh, Won Moo and Kim, Kwang Chung (1984). *Korean immigrants in America*. P.74 Associated University Press.

In addition to the reconceptualization of assimilation along the lines of social and economic assimilation, there was a concomitant interest in the issue of residential mobility; a determinant of spatial assimilation. Douglas Massey (1985)[24] formalized the significance of residential mobility and residence for understanding the assimilation paradigm. He viewed spatial distribution of racial and ethnic groups as a reflection of their human capital and as a tool to gauge the state of their assimilation. Essentially for Massey residential mobility follows from acculturation. Social and residential mobility of ethnic families is perceived as an intermediate step on the way to structural assimilation. Ethnic and racial minorities are perceived as moving in the direction of assimilation (structural) to the extent that their educational, occupational, income and residential characteristics approached, or exceed those of Anglo Americans or native-born non-Hispanic whites. Findings of persistent inequality in life chances were interpreted as evidence of discrimination and restrictions on the opportunity for assimilation. Massey's theoretical understanding of the ethnic and racial barriers to structural assimilation clearly resonates with the work of Royster.

Royster (2003)[25] critiqued the socio-economic assimilation theory in her text: *"Race and the Invisible Hand."* Royster through a qualitative methodological design disproved the myth of a level playing field and equal life chances for competent individuals belonging to ethnic groups. Her contention is that racial stratification and the accompanying lack of significant networks are the primary limiting processes creating real-life barriers to economic mobility and socio-economic assimilation. Royster's work emphasizes the inter-section of immigration, race and class stratification in her depiction of ethnic and racial adaption.

Finally, Shibutani and Kwan (1965)[26] formulated a sophisticated theoretical analysis of ethnic stratification and assimilation based on symbolism and meaning that the majoritarian culture attributed to a specific immigrant group. It is this symbolic meaning that creates varying social distance between mainstream society and the immigrating ethnic group. Shibutani and Kwan state that how a person is treated in society depends not on what he is but how he is identified, racially and ethnically. People are categorized (by race and ethnicity) and interacted with based

---

[24] Massey, Douglas (1985). Ethnic residential segregation, *Sociology and Social Research* 69, pp. 356-364.
[25] Royster, Deirdre (2003). *Race and the invisible hand.* University of California Press.
[26] Shibutani, Tmoatsu and Kwan, Kian (1965). *Ethnic stratification.* Macmillian, p. 39 and pp. 263-271.

upon preconceived behaviors. This enables individuals, on a manifest level, to deal with primary group non- members in a routine and predictable manner; and on a latent level it creates and supports a system of racial and ethnic based stratification. This categorization of others into ethnic and racial groups stems from the cognitions constructed in social interactions in both the public and private sphere and not biologically substantiated differences. Social distance, a subjective sense of nearness to a group, is the key concept in the creation of the color line that segregates minorities and impedes assimilation In their account, change in the individual's subjective sense of closeness leads to a reduction of social distance, which both precedes structural assimilation and stimulates it occurrence. Shibutani and Kwan stress that the mechanisms that bring about the reduction of social distance originate in structural/institutional changes that occur at a macro level. In the absence of macro level changes, ethnic stratification categories are stable and the segregation of racial minorities into ethnic enclaves and the creation of systemic barriers of stratification persist indefinitely.

Section 3:
Conclusion

Alba and Nee suggest the need for the continued construction of new theories of assimilation in our post- modern world; theories that can recognize the salience of agency in the individual and the power of institutions. According to Alba and Nee, institutional theories evolved from of two distinct traditions. The first is the methodological individualism of Max Weber's comparative institutional analysis. Weber (1930/1958)[27] in his seminal text: *"The Protestant Ethic and the Spirit of Capitalism"* is the often cited example of the use of context bound rationality in explaining institutional change. His theory purports that the actions of individuals stem from their religious beliefs (world view) which in turn are causal mechanism for their actions. The second tradition is the methodological holism of Emile Durkheim which asserts that institutional structures cannot be reduced to the action of individuals. These opposing theoretical traditions have moved in the direction of convergence; integrating purposive action with large-scale institutional processes. According to Alba and Nee (2003:37)[28], *"these new convergent*

---

[27] Weber, Max (1904-1905). *The Protestant ethic and the spirit of capitalism.* trans. Talcott parsons, Charles Scribner's Sons 1958.
[28] Alba and Nee, p.37, ibid.

theoretical approaches, view institutional change as being embedded in the purposive actions of individuals, which in turn are shaped by cultural beliefs, relational structures."

For Alba and Nee (2003:37)[29] the contemporary theory for the deconstruction of the adaptive processes of acculturation and assimilation is Weberian in conceptual style and views agents acting in accordance with mental models shaped by cultural beliefs, customs, social norms, ideology and religion that mold perceptions of self-interest; *"Individuals follow rule of thumb heuristics in solving problems and make decisions in the face of uncertainty stemming from incomplete information."* Here rationality is context bound and focuses analytic attention on integrating the decision paths for choices made by individuals within an analysis of macro level context. I interpret Alba and Nee's position as recognizing the significance of subcultural identities as tools that the immigrant utilizes in attempting to negotiate their new environment successfully. This conceptualization of the assimilation or change process is at the core of this study.

---

[29] Alba and Nee, p.39, ibid.

CHAPTER THREE

IMMIGRATION AND RELIGIOUS PRACTICE

Chapter Overview

I have captured in the preceding chapter the expanding theoretical conceptualization of the process of immigrant adaptation and indirectly the life-world demands that immigrants must address. It should be evident that my understanding of the process of acculturation and assimilation is itself context bound and reflective of society's receptivity to a re-conceptualization of immigrant adaptation.

According to Yang and Ebaugh (2001)[1] immigration scholars will for the foreseeable future continue their conversation as to whether or not the post1965 immigrant will adapt to US society with the same pace and in the same fashion as the early periods of immigration. However what poses less of a question is the significance of religion and religious institutions in the process of acculturation and assimilation. Religion and religious institutions have been among the most important and consistent resource that immigrant groups have used to reproduce there ethno- religious identity and create support for the immigrant in their challenging adaptation to the new environment. Chapter three will present a brief overview of the relationship between the immigrant and their religious practices within the context of assimilation.

Section 1:
The Relationship between Immigration
and Religious Practice

Historically religion has functioned as a tool to mediate tensions created by ethnic and cultural differences between established groups and new comers. This is certainly true for the post 1965 immigrant. Religious

---

[1] Yang, Fenggang and Ebaugh, Helen Rose (2001). Transformation in new immigrant religions and their global implications, *American Sociological Review,* v.66, N.2., pp. 269-388.

differences in the United States are the most significant differences our society permits (Warner 1998) and a valid form of expressing ethnic differences (Casanova).[2] Religion can be viewed as a psychological and sociological construct as well as a public space for immigrant group's to develop a public voice. Religion can function as an institution creating social structure and as a system creating meaning through symbolic action. As an institution creating social structure, religious organizations can take on the necessary and supportive role of a social service agency assisting immigrants with secular concerns (economics, educational issues and political action). Historically, researchers addressing the relationship of religious institutions to immigration stress the social- economic and political effects of religious institutions on the lives of immigrants (Foner and Alba 2008).[3] When viewed as a system of meaning making, religion has provided immigrants with symbolic interpretation of the experience of immigration, reinforcement of ethnic identity through ritual practice and support for both individual and collective self-esteem (Alba and De Wind 2009[4]: Orsi 1985).[5]

Before 1990 few sociologists were concerned with the religious beliefs, practices, or organizations in the lives of post1965 immigrants. Those who did focused primarily upon the functional roles of religious organizations; how they provided social services to members and how they facilitated or hindered the processes of assimilation and acculturation for immigrants.

Beginning in the early 1990s many sociologists have conducted research about the religious lives of post1965 immigrant. These studies demonstrated that the relationship between religion and immigration is extraordinarily complex and significant. The early research emphasized religiously-based migration to the United States and the development of congregations (Warner and Wittner 1998).[6] Authors (Yang and Ebaugh 2001[7]; Bankston and Zhou 2000)[8] hypothesize that "congregationalization"

---

[2] Cassanova, Jose (1994).Public religions in the modern world. University of Chicago Press.

[3] Foner, Nancy and Alba, Richard (2008). Immigrant in the United States, *International Migration Review*, 42:360-392.

[4] Alba, Richard and DeWind, Josh (2009). *Immigration and religion in America: Comparative and historical Perspectives*, New York University Press.

[5] Orsi, Robert (1985). *The Madonna of 115th St.: Faith and community in Italian Harlem.* Yale University Press

[6] Warner, Stephen and Wittner, Judith (1998). *Gatherings in diaspora*. Temple University Press.

[7] Yang, and Ebaugh, ibid.

or the process of adopting a congregational form and organizational structure was one of the central processes that contributed to the transformation of immigrant's religion in contemporary United States and facilitated their adaptation in the United States .

Warner theorized that there are five principles that need to be considered when analyzing the relationship between religion and immigration. I will use Warner's (2000)[9] theoretical approach to structure and thematically develop this chapter.

Warner posits five principles that are essential to our understanding of the relationship between religion and immigration: 1) the salience of religion to immigrants; 2) migration is not random with respect to religious tradition; 3) individual and collective identities are not static; 4) religion in the United States is subject to the process of congregationalism; 5) congregations themselves become a venue for inter-group and intra-group dynamics. I will address and expand upon each of these five principles as a means of deconstructing the relationship of religion and immigration.

Religion for the immigrant is salient for multiple reasons in the process of assimilation. The first reason is self- reflection. Smith (1978)[10] gives us that immigration promotes reflection on the meaning of a group's history and why they are part of the migration process. For Smith as well as Durkheim (1973)[11] and Weber (1961)[12] religion and ethnicity are intertwined in contemporary societies. Religion regulates behavior, legitimizes power, transforms group memory into ideology and gives social meaning to the collective and individual lives of group members. Religious and communal rituals assist the immigrant in their adaption to the host society by supporting their self-reflection of the assimilation process. Expanding upon and taking some liberty with the work and perhaps intent of Geertz (1963)[13] immigrants through their religious traditions are able to hold together their view of the right ideals for life and their worldview of social reality as they adapt to the new.

---

[8] Bankston, Carl and Zhou,Min (2000). De facto congregationalism and social economic mobility in Laotian and Vietnamese immigrant communities, *Rev. Relig. Res.*, 38: 18-37.

[9] Warner, Stephen (2000). Religion and new immigrants: Some principles drawn from field research, *American Studies*, 41: 267-286.

[10] Smith, Timothy (1978). Religion and ethnicity in America, *American Historical Review* 83: 1155-1185.

[11] Durkheim, Emile (1973). *On morality and society: Selected writings*, edited Robert Bellah, Chicago, 222-2 23.

[12] Weber, Max (1961). Ethnic groups; In Parsons, *Theories of society*, 305-309.

[13] Geertz, Clifford (1963). *Old societies and new states*. New York, 90-114.

Preservation of ethnicity is a significant issue for immigrant families experiencing the process of adaptation and the second reason for the salience of religion to immigrants. Religious institutions act as free social spaces under the American system of religious disestablishment. Unlike the immigrants experience in the public sphere (workplaces and schools), immigrants in their own places of worship are not subject to majoritarian pressure to speak English and conform to American mainstream ways. Immigrants find in religious institutions a supportive environment that reminds them of home and allows them a place to practice and reinforce their ethnicity. Religious rituals especially those practiced in congregations become a major mechanism for preserving ethnic culture and identity across generations (Min 2010).[14]

For many immigrants, especially the post1965 immigrant males, a loss of social and economic status accompanies immigrating to the United States. The social roles that are made available to them in their religious communities are compensatory and become an additional salient factor. Holding a church office can help them reclaim honor denied in the host society. Election to church offices is viewed as status honor and often the source of serious contention. Sheba George(1998)[15] in her article *"Caroling with the Keralites: the Negotiation of Gendered Space in an Indian Immigrant Church"* captures the significance of church status for male Indian immigrants as well as the intergenerational and gender struggle for status within a religious institution.

Finally religion is salient due to its ability to address inter-generational tensions that accompany acculturation and assimilation. The 1.5 and second generation can experience the demands of acculturation in ways different from the immigrant generation. Participating in a different religious tradition from the immigrant generation or developing a new religious perspective can assuage intergenerational tensions. Evangelical Christianity or being born again, can facilitate and ease the break for the Korean second generation from their parents culture that their mobility aspirations demand (Yep et al., 1998[16]; Min, 2010).[17]

Immigration is not random with respect to religion. Bashi (2007)[18] has documented the significance of networks and pre-existing resources in

---

[14] Min, Pyong Gap, ibid.

[15] George, Sheba (1998). *Caroling with the Keralites: Negotiation of gendered space in an Indian immigrant church.* In Warner and Wittner, eds., 265-293.

[16] Yep, Jeanette et al.,(1998). *Following Jesus without dishonoring your parents.* Downers Grove, Ill.

[17] Min, Pyong Gap, ibid.

[18] Bashi, Francine (2007). The survival of the knitted, Stanford University Press.

migration and Warner underscores this significance with his concept of "push and pull factors". A pull factor for Warner, being the presence of welcoming co- religious and co-ethnics who may be able to provide employment in the host country and a push factor being the existence of targeted persecution, discrimination, and poverty towards a particular religious or ethnic group in their country of origin. Thus, immigrants who come to the United States often represent a religiously and at times social and economically skewed sample of the population of the sending country.

For example South Korea is approximately 25% Christian but 50% of the immigrants from that country to the United States are Christian at the time of immigration and half of the remainder join Christian churches as they settle into the United States. Thus some 75% of Korean immigrants in the United States are Christian (Kwon 2001).[19] Vietnam is a Buddhist country with a Christian minority. However a high portion of Vietnamese immigrants are Catholic immigrating partially due to political repercussions from the Communists victory (Bankston and Zhou 1996).[20]

The complexity of deconstructing the migration process is further added to by the internal workings and ethnic boundaries within the sending countries themselves. According to Warner (2000)[21] one of the important categories of immigrants who came as a result of the occupational preference provision of the 1965 law were nurses from such sending countries as Philippines, Korea and India. In India Christians tend to be concentrated in states like Kerala, with its high levels of education. Christian women are less likely to be subject to Hindu based strictures against 'polluting" occupations. Indian nurses therefore are very likely to be Christian women from this geographic area adding to both religious and gender diversity (George1998).[22]

Identities are not static. Individual and group identity formation, the ways individuals think of themselves and their relationships to others is an essential theme in our analysis of religion and immigration (Cerulo1997).[23] Religious identities are constructed on the basis of sending country material and group alignments in the receiving country. In other words what you were in the sending country (identity) is not what you will

[19] Kwon, Ho-Young and Kwang, Chung Kim (2001). *Korean American religion: Pilgrims and missionaries from a different shore*. University Park, PA.
[20] Bankston, Carl and Zhou, Min (1996). *The Ethnic church, ethnic identification, and the social adjustment of Vietnamese adolescents*, Rev. Relig. Res., 38; 18-37.
[21] Warner, Stephen, ibid.
[22] George, Sheba, ibid.
[23] Cerulo, Karen (1997). Identity construction: New issues, new directions, *Annual Review of Sociology*, 23: 385-409

necessarily be or become in the host country. Identities are many sided, fluid and shaped by over lapping historical and social contexts (Ajronch 2004).[24]

Kurien (1998)[25] suggests that religious identities become more salient for immigrants in the United States than in their nations of origin because of the role religions play in preserving ethnic identities. This appears to changes with the second generation. Cadge and Ecklund (2006)[26] argued that second-generation immigrants are less religious than their parents and that it may not be until the third generation that immigrants returned to their religious roots as a way of ethnic identification (Chai1998[27]; Kwon et al., 2001).[28] Min and Kim (2005)[29] in a small research study conducted with the Korean community in New York City, report that about two thirds of the adults they surveyed, who attended a Korean church as children participated in church as adults. More than two thirds of those attended a Korean Congregational church. Many second-generation Korean Americans are more identified with Evangelical Christianity then with Korean ethnicity as indicated by their preference to marry an Evangelical Christian even if they were not of Korean ethnicity (Min 2010).[30] Indians (Asians) in the United States attempt to project a religious identity rather than one that locates them in the American racial hierarchy corresponding to the color of their skin (Kurien1998).

The issue of individual agency in the process of creating religious identities is also significant. Ng (2002)[31] in his work with Chinese immigrant churches argues that the process of converting to a mainstream religion in the United States involves Chinese immigrants developing their own appropriations of culture, symbols and practices even though they are

---

[24] Ajrouch, KJ.(2004). Gender, race and symbolic boundaries. *Sociological Perspectives*, 47: 371-39.

[25] Kurien, P.(1998). Becoming American by becoming Hindu, In Warner.and Wittner editors, *Gatherings in Diaspora*, 37-70

[26] Cadge, W. and Ecklund, EH. (2006). Religious service attendance among immigrants: Evidence from new immigrant survey-pilot, *American Behavioral Science*, 49: 1574-1595.

[27] Chai, KJ. (1998). Competing for the second generation: In Warner and Wittner, editors, *Gatherings in diaspora*, 295-331.

[28] Kwon, et al., ibid.

[29] Min, Pyong Gap and Kim, DY (2005). Intergenerational transmission of religion and culture: Korean Protestants in the United States, *Sociology of Religion*, 66: 263-282.

[30] Min, ibid.

[31] Ng, KH (2002). Seeking the Christian tutelage, *Sociology of Religion*, 63: 195-214.

converting to Christianity and institutionally accepted religion in the United States. Yang (2000)[32] states: *"that religious and ethnic identities are not an either or matter of assimilation or cultural retention. Rather identities for Chinese are best described as adhesive, allowing for both selective assimilation and selective preservation of ethnicity in the process of negotiating what it means to be Christian, American, and Chinese.*

It is evident that religious identity is more than either achieved or ascribed; it is a negotiated construct with race being both a conditioning factor as well as condition in the negotiation process. Religious identities change over time as immigrants and following generations adapt to US culture. This is captured in Min's work (1992)[33] and his study of first generation Korean churches which demonstrated that the preservation of ethnic traditions and customs is a main function of Korean religious centers. His later analysis (Min 2010) of Indian Hindus and Korean Christians demonstrated how religious organizations help both groups preserve ethnic tradition by making religious and ethnic rituals synonymous. It also captures how the relationship between the individual and religion changes from the immigrant generation to 1.5 and second generation; more so for some ethnicities (Korean) than others. This later text makes the observation that the relationship between religion and ethnicity can take different trajectories in the process of adaptation. There would appear to be multiple pathways for the immigrants to use religion in the process of identity construction. The utilization of religion to construct a religious identity, to facilitate development or retention of an ethnic identity or a combination of both is dependent upon the unique civil and cultural context that an immigrant group is situated within and the social and economic capital they possess.

Religion in the United States is subject to the process of congregationalism, a form of church governance or organization, based upon a local collective, where each congregation is independent and autonomous in running its own affairs. Regardless of how a religion may be organized in the sending country there is a tendency for religious institutions in the United States to develop a congregational form of structure. Congregationalism in the United States is the preferred form of

---

[32] Yang, F. (2000). Chinese gospel church, In Ebaugh and Chafez editors, Religion and the new immigrants, Alta Mira Press 89-107.
[33] Min, Pyong Gap (1992). The structures and social functions of Korean immigrant churches in the United States, *International Migration Review*, 26:1370-1394.

religious organization and immigrant religious institutions take on a de-facto form of congregationalism (Warner1994[34]; Warner 2000).[35]

Numerous studies have been conducted on Congregationalism in immigrant churches and the various forms and purposes it may undertake (Ebaugh and Chafetz 2000[36]; Warner and Wittner 1998).[37]) In a study titled *"Tenacious Unity in a Contentious Community: Cultural and Religious Dynamics in a Chinese Christian Church"*, Yang (2000) analyzed tensions within the Protestant Chinese Fellowship Church, a non-denominational evangelical church which provides its highly educated, middle class professional Chinese membership with a broad range of both religious and ethnic activities. Yang found that in this congregation, the congregational church structure was helpful in mediating the tension created by the clash of civilizations; Christian religion and Chinese culture.

In a somewhat different fashion, Kurien (1998) wrote about Malayalee speaking Hindus in southern California. Her intent was to demonstrate how religion sustains ethnic life in the Hindu community. How becoming Hindu has been an essential part of Asian Indians adaptation to the United States and an essential part of their journey from immigrants to citizens.

Finally Bankston and Zhou (2000)[38] conducted a comparative analysis of two Southeast Asian religious organizations. One a Vietnamese Catholic immigrant churches the other a Laotian Buddhist temple. The authors provide a detailed study of how ethnic communities give rise to immigrant ethnic congregations and facilitate adaptation to the host environment.

Warner and Wittner (1998) in their introduction to the text *"Gatherings in Diaspora"* are clear that if we are to understand the post 1965 immigrant community then we must discover what the new ethnic communities are doing together religiously and what manner of religious institutions they are developing *"of, by, and for themselves"*. We must come to understand the role of immigrant congregations and their relationship to immigrant adaptation. Warner and Wittner make the claim that by studying congregations, we are giving recognition to the fact that religion exists in a living community and that the process through which a

---

[34] Warner, Stephen (1994). The Place of the congregation in the American religious configuration. In New perspectives in the study of congregations, volume 2, edited by Wind and Lewis,Chicago.
[35] Warner, Stephen, ibid.
[36] Ebaugh and Chafetz, ibid.
[37] Warner and Wittner, ibid.
[38] Bankston and Z hou, ibid.

religion takes on the manifestations of a specific immigrant group is by necessity, ongoing and fluid.

Congregations are themselves a venue for inter-group dynamics. Congregations (religious institutions) are locations where relationship dynamics between gender and immigrant generational cohorts can be negotiated. Bankston and Zhou (1996) view immigrant churches as locations where the second-generation can negotiate their relationship with the first generation while creating cultural and social capital that leads to economic and educational assimilation The 1.5 and second generations of most new immigrant groups are acculturating rapidly and thereby creating an immigrant generational gap. We can expect generational conflict because the immigrant generation desires religious institutions and rituals to remain formal and be reminders of their country of origin. This is not an issue for the new second-generation immigrant cohort, who often views immigrant religious activities and rituals as alien (Chai1998[39]; 2001).[40]

Gender relations in immigrant churches are another dynamic issue that creates tension. In many immigrant churches there is strong disagreement over the role that women should play in religious rituals and its institutional management. This disagreement reflects contention over status and power. One way that the second generation and their religious institutions differ from the immigrant generation and their churches is the higher status assigned to women in formal religious roles. Ebaugh and Chafetz (1999)[41] claim that: *"to the extent that male congregants perceive themselves to have suffered status loss in the process of immigration, they try to recoup their sense of worth through incumbency in prestigious congregational roles."* This leaves little space for women to hold roles of authority within the immigrant churches system. Reconfiguring gender roles within the immigrant church structure is a second issue that requires negotiation.

Conclusion

One can argue that the integration of the post 1965 immigrant cohort is occurring, because immigrants are adjusting their beliefs and practices, socializing with neighbors and co- workers, who for the most part accept

---

[39] Chai, ibid.
[40] Chai, KJ. (2001). Beyond strictness to distinctiveness: generational transition in Korean Protestant churches, See Kwon et al., *Korean Americans and their religions*. University Park: Penn State University's 2001, 295-331.
[41] Ebaugh, Helen and Chafetz, Janet (1999). Agents for cultural reproduction and structural change, *Social Forces*, 78, 608.

immigrant ethnicity and religious differences (Albanese 2000).[42] In order
to answer question: "are *members of the post1965 immigrant cohort being
integrated into the wider society"*, we need to consider the issue of social
integration.

Social integration can be viewed as phenomenological in approach
emphasizing the meaning of practices and beliefs in immigrant groups;
how immigrants construct individual and collective identities. It stresses
the processes by which lifestyles and self -perception change the pathways
of resistance and accommodation that occur within immigrant groups
(Geertz 1973[43]; Wuthnow and Hackett 2003).[44] Complementary to the
phenomenological view of social integration is the structural approach
which emphasizes social resources and the broader social networks in
which immigrant group become embedded: in this perspective immigrant
groups interact with the wider society, construct and occupy social niches,
compete with other immigrant groups in the development of identity in
relation to structures of power (Yang and Ebaugh 2001).[45]

Although the laws and civil norms addressing religious freedom,
tolerance and respect for human rights make it possible for immigrants to
be accepted as part of civil society, the degree to which immigrant groups
become fully integrated into the society depends not only on public
tolerance but also on the resources they have at their disposal. Social
capital (phenomenological and structural), are the resources that the
immigrant can mobilize to become integrated into a host society and create
bridges to the wider society. Attaining higher education, achieving a
sufficient income, social prestige and participating in the political process
are the principal bridges new immigrant groups have to build these
networks and become socially integrated. It is clear that religion both
symbolically and institutionally, plays a significant role in the production
of social capital which is essential for the immigrant's social integration
into mainstream civil society. It provides access for the immigrant into the

---

[42] Albanese, C.L.(2000). The culture of religious combining: Reflections for the
new American millennium, *Cross Currents*, 50: 16-22.
[43] Gertz, Clifford (1973). The interpretation of cultures. New York: Basic Books.
[44] Wuthnow, Robert and Hackett, Conrad (2003). The social integration of
practitioners of non-western religions in the United States, *Journal for the
Scientific Study of Religion* 42:4, 651-667.
[45] Yang, F and Ebaugh, H (2003). Transformations in new immigrant religions and
their global implications, *American Sociological Review*, 66:269-288.

public sphere of civil life and facilitates the creation of political, economic and social capital in the public sphere (Foley and Hoge 2007[46]).

---

[46] Foley, Michael and Hoge, Dean (2007). *Religion and the new immigrants: How communities form our newest citizens.* Oxford University Press.

CHAPTER FOUR

THE RELATIONSHIP BETWEEN RELIGION AND POLITICS IN THE UNITED STATES

Chapter Overview

Chapter 4 presents a deconstruction of the relationship between religion and politics through a conversation addressing the role of belief, practice and belonging in the religious- political equation. I will close this chapter by taking the position that culture, specifically subcultural identity, is a viable bridge between religion and politics.

Section 1:
Religion and Politics: Private or Public Sphere

The boundary between religion and politics is often gray, but the presence and power of religion in civil society and our culture of democracy has never been questioned. Tocqueville in his visit to the United States shortly after its founding was struck by the pervasiveness of religion and referred to religion as the first of American institutions (Bryant 2005).[1] Religion in the United States is characterized by diversity in religious beliefs and practices and a high adherence. According to a recent Pew survey (Pew 2008),[2] 83% of Americans claim to belong to a religious denomination, 40% claim to attend services weekly, and 58% claim to pray at least once a week. The majority of Americans report that religion plays an extremely important role in their lives, which is why the United States is considered one of the most religious countries in the world (Eck2002).[3]

---

[1] Bryant, Clell (2005).Tocqueville's America. *Smithsonian Magazine*, July, 104-107.
[2] Pew Forum on Religion and Public Life, (2008). .U.S.. Religious landscape survey, Pew Research Center, Washington, D.C.
[3] Eck, Diana (2002). A new religious America. Harper One, p 432.

The majority of Americans (76%) identify themselves as Christians, mostly within Protestant and Catholic denominations (ARIS 2008).[4] Based on data in the 2008 American Religious Identification Survey, roughly 51.3% of Americans are Protestants, 25% are Catholic, 1.7% are Mormon and 1.7% are other Christian denominations. Other major faith traditions in the United States include Judaism 1.4%, Buddhism .7%, Islam .6%, Hinduism .4% and a variety of other faiths including Unitarians, New Age groups. Native American religions combine to make up an additional 1.2% of the religious adult population. According to ARIS, 86% of the adults surveyed reported a belief in God with 9% reporting religion being the most important aspect of their life.

Religion as we have seen in Chapter 3 is a multifaceted and multi-purpose phenomenon; for some it provides an explanation of their existence and creates a fundamental meaning in life (Stark and Finke 2000).[5] Fowler (1989)[6] posits that liberalism with its emphasis on autonomy of the individual leaves people without a sense of community and clear standard of behavior. Religion fills this void in our liberal society. Religion promotes a particular interpretation of why things are the way they are, how they ought to be, and what the individual's role is in this world. It provides guidelines for 'right action" (Queen 2002).[7]

Stark and Glock (1968)[8] identified five core dimensions that they believe comprise religion: beliefs, ritual practice, private devotionalism, religious knowledge, and a consequential or ethical dimension. Stark and Finke (2000) propose combining religious institutions and two interconnected components of religious commitment, objective (behavior) and subject (beliefs) in their hypothesis as to what constitutes the essential elements in all religious traditions.

It has been documented that religious Americans use religion in public to rationalize opinions or actions, and to justify political and civil engagement (Casanova 1994).[9] Religion has been used to define collective

---

[4] *American Religious Identification Survey,* (2008), Trinity College, Hartford Connecticut.

[5] Stark,Rodney, and Finke,Roger (2000). *Acts of faith.* University of California Press.

[6] Fowler, Robert (1989). Postmodern biblical criticism, *Foundations and Facets 5:3-30.*

[7] Queen, Edward (2002).Public religion and voluntary associations. In *religion, politics and the American experience,* Ed. Blumhofer, University of Alabama Press, pp. 86-102.

[8] Stark, Robert and Glock, Charles (1968*). American piety.* University of California Press

[9] Casanova, ibid.

identities and to map both the individual's and the group's place in civil society (Lichterman 2008).[10] Religious community service and social activist organizations provide a broad array of services to the religious and are in essence civic groups functioning in the public sphere. They often are voluntary, can be either formal or informal and act independently of the state and the imperatives of market exchange (Cohen and Arato 1992).[11]

From a theoretical perspective there are several paradigms that have been utilized to explain the linkage between religion and politics. The ethno- religious perspective exemplified by Durkheim, which focuses upon religion as a social phenomenon and emphasizes affiliation (belonging) with religious groups as the means by which religion shapes political responses. Theorists such as Durkheim, Marx and Parsons understood social structures and institutions as consisting of social regularities and objective patterns external to individual action and intentions and not reducible to the sum of those actions. These theorists subscribed to macro social theories in which *"the major explanatory variables were larger structural phenomena. The behavior of individual actors was understood to be strongly influenced or even determined by the various structures or institutions of society. The human being as an active agent exercising free will and contributing to his or her circumstances was not a consideration from this perspective"* Kondrat (2002:436).[12]

Pollsters and politicians rely primarily on the ethno-religious perspective for their interpretation of American politics and perceive religious groups as developing their own political culture, fostered by religious leaders, houses of worship, and ethnic religious communities. Religion as a social phenomenon is clearly expressed in its affiliation with local churches, specific denominations, and religious traditions. According to Kohut (2000)[13] affiliations provide an arena in which religion is linked to political issues, parties, candidates and activities. However, in our postmodern society, ascriptive affiliations appear to have diminished. Geographic mobility has led to the American religious moving among religious settings and shifting amongst religious traditions. The validity of

---

[10] Lichterman, Paul (2008). Religion and the construction of civil identity, *Amer. Sociological Review*, v.73, pp. 83-104.
[11] Cohen, Jean and Arato, Andrew (1992). *Civil society*. MIT press.
[12] Kondrat, Mary (2002). Actor centered social work, *Social Work* 47 (4), 435-446.
[13] Kohut, Andrew, et al., (2000).*The diminishing divide*. Brookings Institutional Press.

religion affiliation as a paradigm for understanding the political- religious relationship has become problematic (Ammerman 1997).[14]

The second theoretical perspective, a restructuring prospective, has its roots in the work of Max Weber who saw religion embodied in beliefs and emphasized the role of beliefs in shaping political attitudes and behavior (Smidt, Kellstedt and Guth 2009).[15] For Weber human beings are motivated by ideal and material interests. *"Ideal interests such as the desire to be saved from the torments of hell are also ends oriented, except that these ends are derived from symbolic realities. Interests are the engine of action pushing it along but ideas define the destinations human beings seek to reach and the means for getting there"* Swidler (1986:274).[16]

A third formulation, a synthesis of both the ethno- religious and restructuring theoretical perspectives, combines both religious affiliation and religious beliefs, practice and belongings in a unified paradigm to explain the relationship between religion and American politics As expressed by Layman: *"the substantive content of faith is embodied in religious beliefs which capture the basic worldview of adherence; the practice of the faith is expressed in behavior, and belonging is revealed by affiliation with the religious community, reflecting a conscious recognition of one's membership in a collective or group."*(Layman 2001: 78-87).[17]

Our understanding of religion must address the salience of religious practice or behavior. There are two aspects of religious practice: public ritual observance such as attendance at worship services and private devotional practices such as prayer or bible reading (Stark and Glock 1968).[18] Similar to beliefs, religious practices can vary by tradition. Although attendance at worship service is usually normative, some traditions put greater emphasis on such participation and expectations on the conduct of congregational worship may vary. For example in white Protestant churches, services rarely go beyond one hour; whereas in black Protestant tradition, services can last throughout the day. In addition the style of service can differ drastically from one tradition to another. *"Some following a set liturgical order while others are much more experiential*

---

[14] Ammerman, Nancy (1997). *Congregation and community*. Rutgers University Press.
[15] Smidt, Corwin, Kellstedt, Lyman and Guth, James, ibid.
[16] Swidler, ibid.
[17] Layman, Geoffery (2001).*The great divide*. Columbia University Press.
[18] Stark and Glock, ibid.

and go where the spirit may lead them" (Smidt, Kellstedt and Guth 2009, p23).[19]

The salience of religion to the individual is frequently viewed as a measure of religiosity. Consequently researchers of religion often conceptualize religious practice in terms of religious commitment, combining frequency of public ritual and practice with private devotionalism and religious salience (Kellstedt et al., 1996[20]: Layman 2001, p.57[21]). These three constructs believing, behaving, and belonging, provide a useful paradigm for analyzing the relationship between religion and politics and will be utilized as the building blocks for this text's construct of religious orthodoxy.

For Stark and Glock (1968)[22] beliefs are central to any understanding of religion and theology and religious belief is at the heart of all faith. Religion embodies fundamental beliefs, ideas and ethical codes and symbols associated with religious tradition. These beliefs have social consequences as people act politically, economically and socially in keeping with their ultimate beliefs. According to Swierrenga:*"Their values, mores and actions are an outgrowth of god or gods that they hold as the center of their being"* (Swierenga 1990: 147).[23] For restructuring theorists, beliefs provide the critical link between religion and politics. The essential questions being which beliefs are central to this paradigm? Where are they located?

Religious traditions have different foundational beliefs and normative practices that constitute their traditional beliefs and behaviors for their members (Green 2000).[24] If restructuring theorists (worldview) are correct, theological differences cross the boundaries of religious tradition. In theory, it may be possible to identify certain beliefs and behaviors that are characteristic of most if not all religious traditionalists. One might expect that traditionalists for example, regardless of specific denomination, would hold that there is a God and believe in an afterlife. In addition traditionalists should agree that there are absolute standards of right and

---

[19] Smidt, Kellstedt and Guth, ibid.

[20] Kellstedt, Lyman et. Al., (1996). Grasping essentials. *In religion and culture wars,* ed. Green et. Al., Rowman and Littlefield, 174-192.

[21] Layman, ibid.

[22] Stark, Robert and Glock, Charles (1968*). American piety.* University of California Press

[23] Swierrenga, Brian, et. Al., (1990). Ethno- Religious political behavior, In *religious and American politics,* ed. Noll, 145-171.

[24] Green, John (2000). Religion and politics in the 1990's. In *The 2000 Eeection in context,* ed. Silk, 19-41, *Center for the Study of Religion In Public Life,* Hartford, Conn.

wrong determined by transcendent authority not by human convention. Such commonalities in beliefs would be important if traditionalists from various religious faiths are unified political as the restructuring model would predict (Hunter1991).[25]

American religious have been characterized as using polarized religious discourse to fight "culture wars" over social issues (Hunter1991).[26] Hunter developed a vision of a religious divide in which he described American religious elites as becoming divided into competing camps; each based upon mutually antagonistic moral visions. In one camp are the culturally Orthodox, those committed to a literal and transcendent conception of authority. This group is comprised of Fundamentalists and conservative Evangelical Protestants along with traditional Catholics and Orthodox Jews. In the other camp are found cultural progressives or modernists consisting primarily of liberal Protestants, Catholics and Jews all of whom see moral authority as more rational and subjective. Hunter's theory concluded that religion in America was not on the brink of collapse but rather in the middle of a divisive crisis.

In summary from a review of the literature, it seems safe to say that belonging, beliefs, and behavior or praxis are all salient variables in explaining the relationship of religion to politics in the American context. However *"attitudes and behaviors correlate only weekly and collections of apparently related ideas and practices rarely cohere into a logical unified mutually reinforcing seamless web"* (Chaves 2010, p.2).[27]

According to Chaves, ideas and practice exists not as a whole but fragmented as bits and pieces. Religious ideas and practices come and go as situations change and develop, producing inconsistencies and discrepancies in life patterns. For Chaves this is true of culture in general and it is certainly true of religious culture. It is with this observation that Chaves introduces the problem or issue of religious congruence.

Section 2:
Culture as a Bridge between Religion and Politics

I will take up the issues of religious congruence and subcultural identity in Chapter 5 in some depth. I would like to present at this point,

---

[25] Hunter, James (1991*). Culture wars*. Basic Books.
[26] Hunter, James (1991*). Culture wars*. Basic Books.
[27] Chaves, Mark (2010). Rain dance in the dry season, *J. for the Scientific Study of Religion*, v49, (1). 2-14.

the opinion that culture can be viewed as a theoretical link between religion and politics (Wald and Leege 2009).[28] I believe that by viewing culture and the creation of subcultural identities as a theoretical bridge between religion and politics our understanding of the relationship between religion and politics is not only enhanced but provides some preliminary answers to the concerns raised by Chaves.

Olson proposes that there are three core aspects defining religion; "*it is a cultural construct, an essential basis of social identity and a multifaceted force of tremendous political significance in today's world*" (Olson 2010, p. 640).[29] It is a well-documented fact that a profound connection exists between religion and culture (Durkheim 1915/1965[30]; Geertz 1973[31]; Leege et al., 2002).[32] It is also well-established that religion is bound up with people's identity and their sense of who they really are (Berger 1967[33]; Greil and Davidman 2007, p. 549).[34]

But how do we understand culture? Geertz (1973: 89, quoted in Ross 1997:301)[35] defines culture as: "*an historically transmitted pattern of meaning embodied in symbols, a system of inherited conceptions expressed in symbolic forms by means of which men communicate, perpetuate, and develop their knowledge about an attitude towards life.*" Olson points out that this definition of culture is useful because it underscores the fact that shared symbolic meaning lies at the heart of cultural and religious systems of meaning. Olson also comments strongly that culture can be too broad a construct to be theoretically useful; especially when culture is perceived as a constant and static force uniting a group of people rather than diverse, fluid and multidimensional. Olson proposes that it is more useful to study differences between and among "*subcultures*" rather than trying to use culture in its broader sense.

---

[28] Wald Brian, et. Al., (2009). The politics of cultural differences. Princton University Press.

[29] Olson, Laura, (2011). The essentials of culrure, *J. for the Scientific Study of Religion*, v50, (4), 640.

[30] Durkheim, Emile (1915/1965*). The elemental forms of religious life*. Free Press.

[31] Geertz, Clifford (1973). Religion and cultural systems. In *the interpretation of culture,* Basic Books, 87-125.

[32] Leege David, et. Al., (2002). *The politics of cultural difference.* Princeton University Press.

[33] Berger, peter (1967), *The sacred canopy.* Doubleday.

[34] Greil, Arthur and Davidman, Lynn (2007). *Religion and identity.* In the Sage handbook of the sociology of religion, eds. Beckford and Demerath, 549-565, Sage.

[35] Ross, mark (1997). The Relevance of culture*, Politics of Psychology*, 1892), 299-326.

Wildavsky (1987:3)[36] adds that culture *"lies at the core of why people want what they want. It is a clear link to political action"*. Again Wildsvsky (1987:5): *"politics arises from social interactions and cultural theory is based on the premise that preferences emerge from social interactions in defending or opposing different ways of life. Applying cultural models to studying politics is not just reasonable but necessary."*

Conclusion

I am in agreement with Olson that culture can be understood as a bridge between politics and religion, but a more specialized concept of culture is required; one of subcultural (identity my word) that will offer more theoretical leverage. Along this line of thought, Leege (2002:13)[37] proposes culture to be a more dynamic construct, anchored in competing notions of how we should and should not live. Such a definition would permit comparisons of the distinctive and at times oppositional ways of life that may exist within a broader understanding of culture. Here culture becomes a tool to achieve ends and not the creator of values that determines what ends are to be sort. Laitin (1988:591)[38] adds clarification: *"to share a culture means to share a language or religion or a historiography. Very rarely do these cultural systems coincide perfectly within a large society. People often must choose which among their religious group, language, and other subcultural identities will be the primary mode of cultural identification in order to maximize life chances."*

Given the above being valid individuals rank order the salience of their subcultural identities or groups to which they belong. Choosing which are most salient at a given moment in creating a sense of self. Most of us respond to messages and symbols that resonate with the core values of the subcultures with which we most fully identify (within a given context and moment in time). An individual's sense of self is multifaceted and fluid; rooted in his or her understanding and prioritization of their salient personal characteristics and values, which are expressed by their most salient group memberships. When an individual has ranked the components of his or her cultural repertoire certain values will take precedence over others (Ross 1997).[39] If politics is the perpetual struggle

---

[36] Wildavsky, Aron (1987). Choosing preferences by constructing institutions, *Amer. Political Science Review*, 81(1): 3-21.
[37] Leege, ibid.
[38] Latin, David (1988). Politics, culture and political preference, *Amer. Political Science Review*, 82(2) :589-593.
[39] Ross, Marc, ibid.

over who gets what, when, and how (Lipperman 1936),[40] then subcultural identity helps individuals decide these issues. *"Subcultural identity determines which symbolic and material objects people considered valuable and worth fighting over, the context in which such disputes occur and the rules by which politics take place"* (Olson 2010: 642).[41] Religion in my opinion is clearly a significant subcultural identity but only one of many and not always the most salient.

---

[40] Lipperman, Harold (1936). *Politics: Who gets what, when, how*. Mcgraw-Hill.
[41] Olsen, ibid.

CHAPTER FIVE

THEORETICAL PERSPECTIVES

Chapter Overview

Immigrant identity appears to change as part of their process of adaptation to the new host environment. The immigrant is not the same individual at the point of migration as when he or she has assimilated into mainstream American society. This study analyzes immigrant identity through a comparative analysis of the post1965 immigrant flow (the first generation or immigrant generational stage, 1.5 generation and 2 generation) and their opinions cast on substantive issues of social and economic concerns. Chapter 5 of the literature review presents an alternative theoretical frame from which to view these changes. I offer two theories, a sub-cultural identity formation and the theory of inter-sectionality, to structure our conversation about the immigrant adaptation process. I will make a case for the significance of context in the process of identity formation and close chapter 5 by differentiating between the constructs of personal identity and the broader construct of social or cultural identity.

Religion matters to immigrants in their accommodation to the new host society; however it is not the only subcultural identity that is present in their adaptation and at times it is not the most salient. I would like to offer an alternative hypothesis to address changes which occur in the immigrant population over the course of their adaptation to a new host country. I propose that what appear to be changes in identity, are in actuality, changes in value of salient subcultural identities, brought about by the everyday demands and decisions that new immigrants face as they assimilate into a new environment.

Section 1:
Shifting Identities: A Case for Context

Religion matters in the formation of identity (Berger 1967)[1] and in the immigrant's adaptation to a new host society (Min 2010).[2] Classical sociology (Weber 1958)[3] makes the case that our religious worldview motivates us and gives justification to our actions. The theory of moral cosmology (Stark and Robinson 2009)[4] continues in this Weberian fashion and attributes identity formation to religious orthodoxy. Specifically, a high degree of religious orthodoxy will lead an individual towards a communitarian stance on economic issues and an authoritarian stance on social- cultural issues. The nonreligious or the non-orthodox religious are seen as modernists by these authors and are perceived as taking stances that are more individualistic on economic issues and moderate/liberal on issues of social-cultural concern.

The principle of religious congruence captures both the power of religion in worldly action and is in keeping with the traditional view of the significance of a religious worldview. In brief it states that an individual's religious ideas constitute a tight and logically integrated network of internally consistent beliefs and values. Actions in both the private and public spheres stem directly from those beliefs and values. Religious beliefs and values are consistently present for the individual and accessible in other life domains. They create a unified schema for the religious and are the foundation for their actions.

If religious congruence is a valid supposition and essential in the process of identity formation, a significant change for example, between immigrant groups along the authoritative – modernist continuum would indicate a co-occurring shift in their identity. Restated, a significant differences in authoritarian – modernist stances between the immigrant generational stage and the immigrant second generation, would be attributable to a significant change in religious identity.

---

[1] Berger, Peter (1967). *The sacred canopy: Elements of a sociological theory of religion.* Doubleday.
[2] Min, Pyong Gap (2010). *Ethnic preservation through religion in America.* University Press.
[3] Weber, Max (1958). *The Protestant ethic and the spirit of capitalisms.* New York; Charles Scribner's.
[4] Stark, Brian and Robinson, Robert (2009). Two approaches to religion and politics: Moral cosmology and subcultural identity, *J. for the Scientific Study of Religion*, 48 (4):650- 669).

Chaves (2010)[5] discounts the principal of religious congruence and indirectly the power of a religious worldview in motivating and justifying our actions in the public sphere. Chaves re-labels the principle of religious congruence as a "religious congruence fallacy" (Chaves 2010:6).[6] He posits that the religious congruency fallacy: " *leads us to search for causal effects we should not be searching for, it leads us to make claims about religious causality that we should not make, and it leads us to posit epicycles to save the religious congruence assumption from evidence that contradicts it."*

There is significant supportive evidence to demonstrate that religious ideas, values and practices are not congruent but are fragmented, compartmentalized, loosely connected, and context dependent (Maio, et. al., 2003[7]: Vaisey 2009).[8]

The concept of "religious incongruence" is readily available in everyday life if we examine instrumental looking ritual and religious action. What we observe is that instrumental ritual and religious action is enacted but supplemental to practical action. This will occur even where the principle of religious congruence would cause us to predict religious action and ritual as being substituted for practical action. For example many religious people believed in divine healing and actively seek healing through prayers and religious rituals. However, very few religious people practice divine healing in place of medical treatment (Wacker 2001:27, 191).[9]

Chaves strongly suggests that religious ideas are present in people's minds but exist contextually. Religious action, including the act of expressing religious beliefs or attitudes in the public sphere, is therefore bounded and situational (Evans-Pritchard 1965:29).[10] It follows then that the use of religious belief and praxis, as motivators and justifies of our actions is contextually limited. The situation or context within which the

---

[5] Chaves, Mark (2010). SSSR Presidential Address, *J. for the Scientific Study of Religion*, 4(1): 1-14.

[6] Chaves, ibid.

[7] Maio, Gregory, et. Al., (2003).Ideologies, values and attitudes. In *the handbook of social psychology*. Ed. Delemater, pp. 283-308, Kluwer Academic Press.

[8] Vaisey, Stephen (2009). Motivation and justification, *Amer. J. of Sociology*, 114(6):1675-1715.

[9] Wacker, Grant (2001). *Heaven below*. Harvard University Press.

[10] Evans-Pritchard, Edward (1965). *Theories of primitive religions*. Clarendon Press.

action occurs is quite possible more important and at times in conflict with the religious disposition (Norenzayan and Shariff 2008: 62).[11]

Mixed results suggesting variability in religious identity appears when we look at religiosity's connection with social – cultural issues i.e. health, political behaviors, sexual behavior, pro-social behaviors, antisocial behaviors, and so forth. For example, Evangelical Protestant and Catholic pregnant teenagers are less likely than Mainline Protestants to seek an abortion. Conservative Protestants are no less likely than other Protestants to be divorced, have viewed an X-rated movie, or to be sexually active even if they aren't married. Decision-making and economic responsibilities in evangelical families are quite different from the ideals that they espouse about the husband being the head of the household (Gallagher and Smith 1999).[12] Research appears clear that religious people do not act in more pro-social ways than anyone else (Batson and Powell 2003)[13] and not always consistently between and within religious traditions.

To summarize, it appears that religious beliefs as a source of motivation and justification are situational specific. Religious practice establishes internalized responses, but because religious practice is situational specific, these automatic responses are themselves situational specific. The fallacy of religious congruence leads us to overlook the reality that in everyday life the powerful and persuasive moods and motivations associated with religion are context bound. According to Hitlin, *"If we want to predict someone's behavior we are better off knowing where they are rather than who they are"* (Hitlin 2008:93).[14] Here I would also add what religious tradition they self identify with.

One can of course contribute this variability in action to an identity change or to religious incongruence. However, if we view religion as only one, albeit a significant sub- cultural identity, then we are open to other subcultural identities being salient for the motivation and justification of action. This is the theoretical position captured in viewing culture as being multifaceted and comprised of sub-cultural identities. It then becomes the individual's task to determine which of the subcultural identities is most salient given the existing situational context and existential demands. It is

---

[11] Norenzayan Ara and Shariff, Azim (2008). The origins of religious pro-sociality, *Science* 322(5898):58-62.
[12] Gallagher, Sally and Smith, Christian (1999). Symbolic traditionalism, *Gender and Society*, 13(2):211-233.
[13] Batson, Daniel and Powell, Adam (2003). Altruism and pro -social behavior. *In Handbook of Psychology*, Wiley, 463-484.
[14] Hitlin, Steven (2008). *Moral selves; Evil selves*. Mcmillian.

not a case of religious incongruence but of shifting salient sub- cultural identification in a continuing process of means attainment.

I believe that Chaves needed to take an additional theoretical step away from religious incongruence and consider this alternative theoretical frame. When applied to immigrants in the adaptive process, variability (in attitudinal stances) between the immigrant generation stage and the 1.5 and second generations is not seen as either an identity change or religious incongruence. It becomes a pragmatic shifting of salient sub-cultural identification, in their attempt to utilize symbolic tools as a normal part of the life process of developing successful problem solving strategies.

I offer this as an alternative hypothesis from which to view these changes between immigrant generations. What appear to be changes in identity, are in actuality, changes in value of salient subcultural identities, brought about by the every- day demands and decisions that the new immigrant faces as they assimilate into a new environment. The following section will present two theories, sub-cultural identity formation and the theory of inter-sectionality to create a supportive frame for this alternative hypothesis for understanding the immigrant adaptation process.

Section 2:
Subcultural Identity Formation
and the Theory of Inter-Sectionality

Subcultural identity theory encompasses the idea that individuals possess multiple, competing group identities that shape their life chances, attitudes and behaviors. Religion or religious subcultural identity is only one of many identity categories that are part of the composite of an individual's identity. These subcultural identities interact to produce mixed and at times unanticipated and contradictory actions (Stryker and Burke 2000[15]; Wuthrow and Llewis 2008).[16]

In effect this study is an attempt to identify the significance of sub-cultural identities on the dependent variables of substantive economic and social concerns relevant in our post- modern world. According to Reed and Eagle (2011)[17] religion is typically viewed as operating in isolation

---

[15] Stryker, Sheldon and Burke, Peter (2000). The past, present and future of identity theory, *Social Psychology Quarterly*, 63(4): 284-297.
[16] Wuthrow, Robert and Lewis, Valerie 92008). Religion and altruistic US foreign policy goals, *J. for the Scientific Study of Religion,* 47(2):191-209.
[17] Read, Jen'nan and Eagle, David (2011). Intersecting identities, *J. for the Scientific Study of Religion*, 50(1): 116-132.

from other bases of social action. Consequently what follows is a conceptualization of a unified straightforward relationship between religious beliefs and outcomes. By focusing upon the relationship between religious beliefs, practice, and one's subjective sense of religiosity and expressed opinions on economic and social issues, at the intersection of gender, religious tradition and immigrant generation stage, I intend to demonstrate that religion's association with attitudes and behaviors is strongly influenced by other social identities. It is my contention that religious subcultural identity does not operate in isolation from other bases of social action such as social class, gender, immigrant generation stage and race.

My theoretical position pulls heavily from the work of Reed and Eagle (2011)[18] who rely on the theoretical perspectives of social identity theory and intersecting social identities. The first, social identity theory, posits that individuals develop their identity from belonging to a group or collective. Individuals belong to multiple groups over their life course. They possess multiple social identities that change and fluctuate over time and context. It is the intersection and competition of these multiple identities that obviously result in what Chaves refers to as religious incongruence and I refer to as shifts in salient subcultural identity.

The second theoretical perspective that of intersecting social identities contends that multiple social inequalities, particularly those based on race, class and gender (to this mix I would add immigrant generation stage), interact to create the social location and life opportunities of groups and individuals and create the intergenerational variability that we observe in immigrant populations (Collins 2005).[19]The utility of the inter-sectionality perspective is that it emphasizes the structural aspect of intersecting identities, and underscores the infinite number of sub-cultural identities that an individual may elect to identify with. The individual's given set of life chances determining which of their sub cultural identities they invoke at a given time and in the different contexts during their life course. These social locations (life chances), some achieved and some ascribed, not only shape beliefs and behaviors but more importantly define which behaviors are viewed as pragmatic and practical at any given point in time. The variability in attitudinal stances which we readily observe arise when the ideas and beliefs grounded in one sub-cultural identity are overshadowed by rituals and behaviors related to another sub-cultural identity that is viewed as being more pragmatic within the given context.

---

[18] Read, Jen'nan and Eagle, David(2011). Intersecting identities, *J. for the Scientific Study of Religion*, 50(1):116-132.
[19] Collins, Patricia (2005). *Black sexual politics.* Routledge.

Section 3:
Additional Thoughts on Identity Formation

According to the anti-essentialist view of personal identity, the prevailing view of social theorists, there is no determinant, de facto, hidden self that reveals itself when conditions are appropriate (Wren 2002).[20] *"Individuals are not born with a master status or a unified set of values that they rely upon to guide their actions"* Reed and Eagle (2011:118).[21] Identities in my opinion are narratives, socially constructed in discourse between individuals and groups within specific historical and institutional contexts.

At this point in my narrative it becomes important to distinguish between the broader construct of identity and the concept of self- person which although intertwined are separate. I offer the following paradigms to demonstrate how identity is possible crafted within a social context.

The first paradigm which I label the ecological paradigm addresses how identity itself is shaped. It is based on the assumption that our psychological states and structures (concepts of self) are formed in the course of social interaction with existing systems and institutions in a recursive process with the individual actor (Wren 2002).[22] Here like Wren, I am not implying that the creation of the self -concept is derived from discourses, such as conversations between friends, or the more significant daily conversations taking place between parents and children within the family. Although significant these conversations are themselves conditional and derived within the context of a larger cultural sphere.

The second paradigm which also relies heavily upon the perspective of social construction addresses not how we think and behave but how our capacities to think and behave have been shaped by our social world. The Feminist discourse that our sexual capacities are themselves socially constructed as well as being gender specific stereotypes are examples of this paradigm. Here: *"the social serves not to mold an antecedently present self or identity, but to bring that self into existence"* (Bakhurst and Sypnowich 1995:6).[23]

---

[20] Wren, Thomas (2002). Cultural identity and personal identity. In *personal and moral identity*, eds Musschenga et.al., Kluwer Academic Press, pp. 231-256.
[21] Read and Eagle, ibid.
[22] Wren, ibid.
[23] Barkhurst, David and Sypnowich, Carol (1995). *The Social self.* Sage publications.

Cross (1985:159)[24] is convinced that the self- person concept does not tell the complete story. He is concerned that personal identity (self-concept) and group identity become conflated. Cross perceived the self-concept or personal identity *"as being an epiphenomenon of social identity or cultural identity, and an amalgam of self-concept and self-esteem."* This then is the third paradigm utilized to understand the role of social construction in identity formation.

For Cross, cultural or social identity, also referred to as group identity, is created within a social and political context. This context is considerably broader than the classical anthropological conceptualizations of culture as a worldview or shared way of life (Geertz 1973).[25] The concept of culture and by implication that of cultural identity *"is no longer understood primarily in terms of world view, shared history, or other aspects of a groups cultural heritage. Culture has evolved into a sociological category so that today one speaks of working-class culture, gay culture, deaf culture, and even the culture of homeless"* (Kincheloe and Steinbert 1997:105).[26]

To add to the complexity of differentiating between personal identity (self- concept) and group identity is the fact that each possesses both a subjective and objective component. A person has both an objective or public component to group identity i.e. being a citizen of the United States and the coexisting subjective or private component to group identity i.e. the affective dispositions, thoughts, intentions and commitments to the group. Wren believes that the objective or public component of group identity is derived from our subjective component or our affective attachment to a specific reference group. It is the social or cultural identity and the accompanying affective component that possesses the power to shape behavior and attitudes. The fact that a person perceives themselves as belonging to a network of human relationships, structured by group boundaries, creates his or her social identity. Finally, the relationship between objective (public) and subjective (private) components of identity is a recursive process; each impacting and giving shape to the other.

The following is taken from Cross (1985; 159)[27] and adds clarity to this complex issue.

---

[24] Cross, William (1985). Black identity. In Spencer et. Al., eds. *The social and affective development of black children*, Hillsdale, 155-171.
[25] Geertz. Clifford (1973). *The interpretation of culture*. New York: Basic Books.
[26] Kincheloe, James and Steinbert, Steven (1997). *Changing multiculturalism*. Open University Press.
[27] Cross, ibid.

Social Identity (cultural or group identity)

Personal Identity   +   Reference Group Orientation

Self-concept (cognitive)
Self-esteem (affective)   ascriptive associations

                                              sub- cultural identities)
                                              racial/class attitudes
                                              gender attitudes
Adapted from Cross, 1985:159

Conclusion

The above paradigm distinguishes between the cognitive and affective components of personal identity as well as capturing the recursive nature of the process between personal identity and reference group orientation. In Cross's paradigm, the reference group orientations are the sub-cultural identities of interest in my study. I believe that the individual's context bound shifts in salient sub-cultural identification, reorders the value of the individual's ritual and practical beliefs and behaviors, bringing about changes in their attitudes and actions.

This work does not discount the importance of religion as an organizing structure in our social life. Religion does matter! Having said this, we also need to attend to how religion interacts with other facets of identity and social location. Read and Eagle (2011:130)[28] admonished: *"we must avoid isolating religion in our analysis and privileging it ad hoc in an attempt to explain and understand complex events"*. This is reasonable advice.

---

[28] Read and Eagle, ibid.

CHAPTER SIX

THEORY OF MORAL COSMOLOGY

Chapter Overview

For the last several decades sociologists of religion have debated whether or not the differences in belief and faith within religious traditions and denominations in the United States have supplanted long-standing differences between them (Hunter 1991[1]; Wutnow 1988).[2] The theory of Moral Cosmology is a major frame for this debate and assumes a religious worldview perspective in that it sees people as differing in their beliefs regarding the locus of moral authority and that these differences have consequences for their politics. The moral cosmology approach focuses on people's beliefs about whether God or individuals constitute the ultimate basis of moral order. This approach contrasts the religiously orthodox to modernists, arguing that the former are theologically communitarian in belief while the latter are individualistic. The communitarianism of the Orthodox is posited to lead to communitarian – authoritarian stances related to modernists on cultural issues of abortion, sexuality, same-sex marriage, divorce and pornography and communitarian /egalitarian beliefs relative to modernists on economic issues. The theory of Moral Cosmology correlates the actions of the religious to their religious orthodoxy and does not attribute action to individual or collective identity associated with religious traditions. Restated, a religiously orthodox person would act in a consistent fashion whether they were Catholic, Protestant, Jewish or Muslim; the driving factor being religious orthodoxy and not identification with a specific religious tradition. Chapter 6 presents the theory of Moral Cosmology, the debate that it was created to address and recent research addressing substantive issues of cultural/ social and economic concern from this theoretical perspective. I offer this section in contrast to the preceding section which presented the theoretical position that identity is comprised of multiple sub-cultural identities giving impetus

---

[1] Hunter, James (1991). *Culture wars*, New York Basic.
[2] Wuthnow, Robert (1988). *The restructuring of American religion*. Princeton University Press.

to our action. For subcultural identity theory religious orthodoxy is only one of many subcultural identities.

Section 1:
The Debate

In his seminal text the *Restructuring of American Religion*, Wuthnow (1988)[3] argued that the symbolic boundaries in American religion have changed in the period since World War II. Denominational antagonism has declined only to be replaced by internecine struggle rooted deeply in educational differences between religious conservatives and religious liberals. According to Wuthnow American religion: *"had split into two camps engaged in symbolic warfare"* (1988:139).[4] The polarization between religious conservatives and liberals was reflected in and exacerbated by the growth of special interest groups intending to effect government action on welfare, education, and civil rights laws. *"This great divide in American religion"* coincided with political divisions in the larger society between conservatives and liberals with theological conservatives taking more conservative political stances than theological liberals on a wide range of social, political and economic issues (Wuthnow 1988: 132, 219-233). Wuthnow (1988:239) argued that *'the political uniformity within each side across a wide range of issues contributed to the public impression of deep polarization between two monolith camps"*.

Hunter (1991)[5] in his book *"Culture Wars"* continued in a like- minded fashion, to further develop Wuthnow's arguments concerning the erosion of denominational antagonisms and the growth of para- Church special interest groups. He postulated a more intractable struggle between the two sides. Hunter (1991:49)[6] argued that; "the *hostilities are so difficult to resolve because they are rooted in fundamentally different conceptions of moral authority"*. On one side the Orthodox believe that God is the ultimate arbiter of what is right and wrong, that the revealed word of God as recorded in sacred texts is inerrant and of timeless relevancy and that God exercises a real and active presence in every-day life. In the Orthodox view, moral standards are absolute, unchanging and universal; moral authority is external and transcendent. On the other side progressives, who include religious modernists as well as nonbelievers and secularists, assert

---

[3] Wuthnow, ibid.
[4] Wuthnow, ibid.
[5] Hunter, ibid.
[6] Hunter, ibid.

that humans are the ultimate arbiters of what constitutes moral action and that the morality of action is publicly contested and should be judged in its cultural context. Individual actors are responsible for their own fates (Hunter 1991:44-45).

Again for Hunter (1991: 42,115) the struggles over a wide range of issues from abortion to affirmative action to what is to be taught in public schools are ultimately rooted in the conflict between Orthodox and progressive moral visions. *"While the association of the religious Orthodox with political conservatism and of the theological progressivism with political liberalism is far from absolute, the relationship between foundational moral commitments in social and political agendas is too strong and consistent to be coincidental"* (Hunter 1991;46). Wuthnow and Hunter suggested a strong degree of uniformity and consensus within each of the sides of the religious division.

Wuthnow and Hunter differed in their perception of the root causes of this religious divide. Wuthnow saw the division as being educationally based while Hunter viewed the division as being rooted in fundamentally opposing moral cosmologies. Yet they were in agreement that there is a divide in American religion between religious conservatives and liberals and that this theological divide coincides with the political conservatives and liberals on a wide range of issues (Davis and Robinson 1996 a: 231).[7]

Despite the fact that competing moral visions are at the heart of today's "cultural wars", Hunter and Wuthnow were clear that public opinion is a complex matter. Public opinions are not always expressed in a coherent, clearly articulated, sharply differentiated worldview. One reason traditionally given as an explanation for this variability is that Scripture itself does not provide an unambiguous basis for taking positions on contemporary issues. Historically, for example, Orthodox Christianity has been associated with pro-slavery and abolition movements as well as with racial segregation and civil rights

Davis and Robinson (1996a:232) noted this variability within the religiously orthodox or conservative groups. They posit that American society, in addition to religious division based upon variability of scriptural interpretations, was also divided along the lines related to gender, race and economic condition. Some groups are likely to benefit from conservative positions on social/economic issues while others are disadvantaged. For religious conservatives to advance a unified front on these issues would require that the self- interest of those that are

---

[7] Davis, Nancy and Robinson, Robert (1996b).Are the rumors of war exaggerated? Religious orthodoxy and progressives in America, *American Journal of Sociology*,102(3):756-787.

disadvantage as a result of conservative policies on gender, race, class and social/economic concerns be superseded by religious authority. Davis and Robinson clearly expect significant differences within the religiously orthodox between men and women on gender issues, between white and people of color on racial issues and between rich and poor on economic issues based upon the above forms of structural stratification. In effect Davis and Robinson are giving credence to the alternative theory of intersectionality.

Moreover Woodrum's research is also supportive of the significance of multiple forms of structural stratification for the motivation and justification of action. He demonstrated that the religiously orthodox or conservative groups draw disproportionately from the disadvantaged; racial and ethnic minorities, the working class, the poor and women (Woodrum 1988:569).[8] Given the demographic composition of the religiously orthodox and the salience of other subcultural identities one would expect that their positions on social/cultural and economic issues are more liberal than the position presented by Wuthnow or Hunter. This I interpret as being supportive of multiple subcultural identities and inter-sectionality as viable explanatory theories for of motivation and justification of our action.

Neither Wuthnow nor Hunter devoted much attention to the possibility of the intersection of religion, race, class or gender as a logical cause of this variability. Hunter and Wuthnow choose to ignore the construct of multiple salient subcultural identities and their inter-sectionality as a viable cause of action and privileged a universal worldview theory.

Section 2:
Taking a Closer Look at the Issue

The prevalent sociological view sees the religiously orthodox as less supportive than moral progressives of women taking on positions that compete with those of wife and mother. They view the religiously orthodox as being opposed to legalized abortion and birth control which make motherhood voluntary, and more opposed to sex education, pornography, homosexuality, and sex outside of marriage, which are seen as separating sexuality from marriage and the task of rearing of children. Concomitantly, this sociological view of the religiously orthodox needs to take into consideration that the conservative attitudes of the religiously

---

[8] Woodrum, Edward (1988).Determinants of moral attitudes „*Journal of the Scientific Study of Religion*, 27: 553-573.

orthodox are often in conflict with attitudinal stances that are motivated and justified by alternative and competing sub-cultural and intersection identity models.

Davis and Robinson (1996b:758)[9] agree that: *"religion is an important source of political division in the United States, but that the major effect of this religious division is on gender, family related issues, sexuality, reproductive rights and woman's involvement in the family and workplace".* They strongly posit that religion independently, is not correlated to issues addressing racial and economic inequality. Here class and racial hierarchies play a far larger role then religious identity and division in creating stances concerning racial and economic justice

Davis and Robinson (1996b: 760)[10] believe that for the Orthodox, issues of sexuality, reproduction, children's schooling, and gender divided labor are inextricably linked to the family and the socialization of the next generation of believers. *"The Orthodox because they hold a conception of timeless and absolute morality that does not compromise with the temporal world are more apt to see themselves as facing a hostile secular world then our moral progressives whose very outlook embraces accommodation to that world".* For the Orthodox, the family is perceived as a bulwark against secular encroachment. A protective umbrella and retreat from the confrontation with a secular world (Ammerman 1987).[11]

We have seen that some research studies are supportive of the position that the religiously orthodox are more conservative than moral progressives on gender and family related issues. However we have also seen that some research studies are not supportive of the position that religious orthodoxy and issues of racial and economic justice are not clearly correlated leaving open the possibility that religious beliefs and rituals intersect with other variables i.e., socioeconomic position, race, gender and here I would add immigrant generation stage to produce the variability in stances or public opinions that we find in the real world.

Traditional and conservative stances are often in opposition to the demands of the every -day world such that the life experience and status interests of the religiously orthodox as a group attempting to defend a timeless moral code and meet the challenges of a changing secular world, are as important as scriptural authority in the formation of their

---

[9] Davis ,Nancy and Robinson, Robert(1996b), ibid.
[10] Davis, Nancy and Robinson Robert (1996b), ibid.
[11] Ammerman, Nancy (1987). *Bible believers: Fundamentalists in the modern world*. Rutgers University Press.

conservative positions on gender and family issues (Gusfield1986[12]: Hill 1989).[13]

Davis and Robinson (1996b:763)[14] suggest two possible explanations for the seeming lack of correlation between religious orthodoxy/ conservatism and racial and economic issues. The first is the ambiguous message of Scripture itself. *"The Bible can mean different things to different people at different times and in different circumstances. There are few ideas in which support a biblical text can be found"*.

The second explanation is based on racial and economic interests. Again according to Davis and Robinson (1996b:763) *"there is no a priori reason to expect that religious conservatism is linked with opposition to racial and economic equality; there is reason to believe that race and socioeconomic position are associated with attitudes towards racial economic inequality"*. Continuing, racial and economic interests would suggest that disadvantaged racial groups and classes are more favorable than advantaged groups towards efforts to reduce inequalities to which they themselves are subject (Robinson and Bell 1978[15]: Davis and Robinson 1991).[16]

The Interest in greater equality of disadvantaged groups among the religiously orthodox affects their religious beliefs leading them to find support in biblical passages for egalitarian ideals. This highlights the intersection of religious identity, race and social class in the creation of a subcultural identity model that is the bases for the motivation and justification of our action. Intersectionality producing the ideological tools applied to the resolution of issues occurring in everyday life.

Davis and Robinson (1996b) capture the significance of race and social economic class in the above identity model. They hypothesize that if this assumption regarding economic and racial interest is correct then the socioeconomic and racial composition of the Orthodox should make them more liberal on racial and economic issues than they would be if they drew equally on all segments of society. Furthermore they hypothesize that in a zero order analysis, without controls for race and socioeconomic variables,

---

[12] Gusfield, Joseph (1986). *Symbolic crusade: Status politics and the American temperance movement*. University of Illinois Press.

[13] Hill, Christopher (1993).*The English bible and the seventeenth century revolution*. Allen Lane, London..

[14] Davis and Robinson, ibid.

[15] Robinson, Robert and Bell, Wendell (1978).Equality, success and social justice in England and the United States. *American Sociological Review* 43:125-43.

[16] Davis, Nancy and Robinson, Robert (1991).Men's and women consciousness of gender equality. *American Sociological Review* 56: 72-84.

the religiously orthodox will be more liberal than moral progressives on questions of racial and economic equality. However with race and socioeconomic variables controlled in both the religiously orthodox and progressive groups, they expect no significant difference between religiously orthodox and moral progressives on racial and economic issues. Here I believe it is quite clear that Davis and Robinson are not only giving full recognition to the significance of other subcultural identities but clearly indicating that race and social class are more salient for justification and motivation of action addressing race and economic issues than religious identity.

In their study titled: *Theological Modernism, Culture, Libertarianism and Laissez-faire Economics in Contemporary European Societies,* Davis and Robinson (2001)[17] analyze the relationship between moral order and individualism in their attempt to deconstruct the theory of moral cosmology and its impact upon cultural and economic attitudes.

They began by citing the work of Kniss (1997)[18] who distinguishes two dimensions of the moral order; one which concerns the locus of moral authority (a transcendent authority or the individual's reason) and the other, the moral project (the community or the individual). The former dimension is at the heart of Hunter's schema addressing the great divide between religious groups. At one poll of this dimension is traditionalism in which emphasis is placed upon a social group defined by its relation to a higher authority. Here: *"Authority transcends any particularities of person, place or time; it is absolute and not open to criticism"* (Kniss 1997:263).

At the other pole is modernism which maintains that the constitutive power for defining ultimate values is grounded in an individual's reason as applied to and filtered through individual experiences; denying traditional transcendent absolute authority. Modernists are theologically individualistic (Davis and Robinson 2001) in that they see individuals as having to provide meaning and purpose to their own lives, as opposed to deriving these from the existence of God. Modernists are individualistic in their belief that individuals themselves and not a deity are responsible for determining the course of their lives.

In supporting modernism as a theologically individualistic moral cosmology to political attitudes, Davis and Robinson following the work of Lipset, Bobbio and Olsen, and propose a two-dimensional structure of

---

[17] Davis, Nancy and Robinson, Robert (2001).Theological modernism: Cultural libertarianism and laissez-faire economics. *Sociology of Religion* 62(1) 23-50.
[18] Kniss, Frank (1987). Culture wars ? *In Cultural Wars in American Politics,* edited by Williams, Aldine De Gruyter, New York.

political beliefs. Lipset (1981)[19] distinguished between cultural conservatism and economic liberalism. The former he believed referred to efforts to restrict freedoms with respect to sexuality, reproduction, schooling and gender roles; the latter addressing efforts to reduce economic inequalities. Bobbio (1996)[20] argued that a left/right dimension (conservative/liberal my words) should refer to positions with regard to the ideal of economic equality; while another dimension liberty/ authoritarianism is needed to locate individuals politically in regards to issues addressing social/ cultural concerns.

Olson (1997)[21] distinguished between personal moral issues and economic justice issues. The former arrays individuals along a dimension of a willingness to allow or restrict individual freedom in matters of personal behavior and is itself an offshoot of Bellah's (1985)[22] "expressive individualism"; the goal being the self-expression of the individual actor. The latter dimension for Olsen concerns the willingness to allow or restrict individual freedoms in the marketplace and is linked to Bellah's "utilitarian individualism" which seeks to maximize the individual's wealth or economic well-being.

In this light economic individualists assume a neoliberal position on economic issues and strongly believe that *"individuals themselves not the communities or larger social structures within which they make their lives determine their economic fates and deserve the credit or blame for whatever outcomes they achieve"* (Feagin 1975).[23]

Economic individualism entails little community or government obligation to the poor and the unemployed. *"The solution to problems of poverty, inequality, and joblessness is not taxation of the rich, government jobs programs to provide work for the unemployed or private charity but greater individual effort by the poor and jobless to help themselves"* (Davis and Robinson 2001:28).

The assumption being that people themselves are in charge and that their destiny is largely in their own hands. *"Some individuals as evidenced by their economic success have exercised their freedom of choice wisely. Others who have failed to succeed have no one to blame but themselves*

---

[19] Lipset, Samuel (1981).*Political man.* Free Press, New York.
[20] Bobbio, N. (1996*). Left and right: The significance of political distinction.* University of Chicago Press.
[21] Olsen, David (1997).Dimensions of cultural tensions among the American public. In *Cultural wars in American Politics,* edited by Williams, Aldine de Grutyer, New York.
[22] Bellah, Robert et. Al. (1985). *Habits of the heart.* University of California Press.
[23] Feagin, James (1975*). Subordinating the poor.* Prentice Hall.

since it was their decision to have acted otherwise (Eisinga 1993: 69).[24]
This ideological posture would be in contrast to a Weberian religious
world view which is quite clear that god plays a role in this equation.

Hunter and Wuthnow privileged moral cosmology as the most salient
sub-cultural identity from which to understand the religious divide and the
resulting motivation and justification for action. Wuthnow differed from
Hunter in that he viewed the root cause of this religious divide as
educationally-based (Davis and Robinson 1996a; 230). Ryle and Robinson
(2006)[25] addressed the issue of the relationship between education and
moral cosmology in their article: *Ideology, Moral Cosmology and
Community in the United States*. This study analyzed the intersection of
two subcultural identities: education and moral cosmology in relationship
to communitarianism. The authors propose that the US educational system
creates an individualistic ideology that disposes highly educated people to
a weaker sense of community. Simultaneously they hypothesize that a
theologically modernist moral cosmology is inherently individualistic
relative to the religiously orthodox cosmology and inclines those holding a
modernist stance to feel less of a sense of community.

Ryle and Robinson begin their argument with the view that the
educational process in the United States is supportive of an individualistic
ideological stance. Their position is not new. Lipset (1981) observed that
well educated people are both more culturally liberal than less educated
people on issues of abortion, reproductive rights, sexuality, school prayer,
civil rights and tolerance in general. Well educated people are more
economically conservative on issues of reducing the economic gap
between the rich and poor, progressive taxation, and job programs.

Stephens and Long (1970)[26] noted that education generally liberalize
people and is associated with more conservative views on economic
issues. Davis and Robinson (1996a) found that well educated Americans
were more liberal on cultural issues and more conservative on economic
issues.

---

[24] Eisinga, Richard et. Al., (1993). Beliefs about the native- migrant socio-economic gap, *Politics and the Individual* 3:67-91.
[25] Ryle, Robin and Robinson, Robert (2006). Ideology, moral cosmology and community, *City and Community*, 5:1, March.
[26] Stephens, William and Long, C. (1970).Education and political behavior, *Political Science Annual* 2, 2-33.

Finally, Phelan (1995),[27] in a study of American attitude towards homelessness found that well-educated people were more tolerant than the less educated toward the homeless but less supportive of economic aid to them.

Ryle and Robinson (2006:54) suggest that what links these bi dimensional stances of the well-educated is a individualistic ideological; *"the well-educated are more culturally individualistic or libertarian than less educated in supporting individual freedom of choice on cultural issues and more economically individualistic or in-egalitarian in expecting the poor to pull themselves out of poverty and in opposing him welfare programs or private charity to reduce poverty".*

Ryle and Robertson (2006:55) continue that it is the content and pedagogy of the educational system in the United States and quite possibly in most post -modern western nations that instills in the student *"a belief in individual freedom of thought over dogmatism, in cultural relativism over absolutism, in competition between individuals over cooperation, and in the attainability of individual upward mobility for self-improvement through education and hard work ".* The individualistic stance created by this educational process is counter to the communitarianism that is found in the theologically Orthodox but congruent with the individualism that has been demonstrated to exist in the theologically modernist position.

The authors summarize that the joint effect of education and a moral orientation are critical in the development of individualistic and communitarian attitudes and view the relationship between the two as complementary and additive. In my perspective, there research clearly demonstrates the intersection of multiple sub-cultural identities (religious identity and educational attainment) as being correlated to attitudes of individualism and communitarianism. Thus both Hunter and Wuthnow were correct in their individual interpretations of the root causes of the religious divide; they were however unaware of their inter-sectionality.

Section 3:
Collective Identity and Politics

Christian Smith (1998)[28] analyzed Protestant religious identities and building upon the work of Wuthnow argued that a variety of subcultural

---

[27] Phelan, James, et., al. (1995).Education, social liberalism and economic conservatism :Attitudes toward homeless people, *American Sociological Review* 60, 126-140.

[28] Smith, Christian, et., al. (1998).*American Evangelicalism: Embattled and thriving.* University of Chicago Press.

religious identities had been created by trans- denominational religious movements and religious entrepreneurs within the Protestant tradition. Smith theorizes that the self identifications of evangelical, fundamentalist, mainline and liberal Protestant were subcultural identities crafted by religious movements that created identity spaces and help develop subcultural communities that supported these identities across Protestant denominations. (Smith 1998:14-15): *"to open up a space between fundamentalism and liberalism in the field of religious collective identity; give that space a name; articulate and promote a resident vision of faith and practice that players in the religious field came to associate with that name and identity space; and fight a variety of religious players to move into that space to participate in the identity work and mission being accomplished their".*

"Research interest in politicized religious identity has been stimulated by the reemergence of the Christian right into politics" (Starks 2009:2).[29] In his article titled: *"Self- identified Traditional, Moderate and Liberal Catholics: Movement-Based identities or Something Else?"* Starks investigates the role of religious movement organizations in the formation of Catholic identities. I take his construct of religious movement organizations to be similar to the theoretical construct of Cross "reference group orientation" which as Cross hypothesized intersects with personal identity in the formation of social/ cultural identity (Cross 1985).[30] Framed in this fashion, Starks is attempting to determine the strength of the correlation

According to Starks (2009:8), Smith saw his theory as an elaboration of the theory of competitive marketing development which emphasized *" how religious entrepreneurs market and sell religious wares or goods, within a religious economy";* creating a view of religious identities as products created and marketed to the religious public by religious movements and elites.

Lindsay (2008; 77-78)[31] in a similar vein focused upon the evangelical movement, and its entry into the "power elite, Para-church organizations", as a central factor in the creation of their religious identity. He concluded that his research demonstrated that evangelical Protestant responders in his study *"were far more loyal to faith based small groups then to particular congregations or denominations".* For Lindsay para church organizations

---

[29] Starks, Brian (2009). Self- Identified traditional, moderate and liberal Catholics, *Qualitative Sociology* 32(1) 1 32.
[30] Cross, William (1985*). Black identity.* Hilsdale, New Jersey.
[31] Lindsey, David (2008).Elite power: Social networks within American Evangelicalism, *American Sociological Review, 73,60-82.*

although not an initial sources of religious identity, are strong mechanisms for integrating networks of disparate evangelicals into a single movement community via the aggregate power of organizations. Such networks according to Lindsay create synergy which flows across domains and develops confirming narratives which reduce symbolic boundaries between religious denominations. Lindsay (2008: 77-78): "as *motivated actors within these overlapping networks interact with one another, they receive further confirmation of the original vision, which first spurred them to action. Through Fellowship experiences within these overlap networks, a sense of shared community is established and cohesive bonds are deepened".*

Again according to Lindsay (2008:79)[32], these confirmatory group narratives are strengthened by the communal experiences within a para - church structure and *"transform individual identities into a cohesive collective identity with the potential to impact the religious field as well as politics, economics and culture".*

Although the significance of religious movements or religious reference group orientations in identity formation has been supported, Starks (2009) wanted to explore the role of religious movements in the formation of identity on an individual level.

His article (Starks: 2009)[33] provided three paradigms which act as links between religious movements and religious self- identity. The first is a "social model" in which religious movement organizations are significant in the developed of religious identities through direct socialization as part of the processes of group membership and participation. The second paradigm posited by Starks and labeled "movement identification" viewed religious movement organizations as not directly socializing members into a religious identity but rather providing institutional resources which help to solidify and articulate the meaning of one's identity. In this model religious identification is indicative of the sense of being a "fellow traveler" with an existing movement. The third paradigm proposed by Starks to address the creation of individual religious identity through collective movements was labeled "generalized cultural conflict model". In this model religious movement organizations do not socialize individuals into their religious identity, nor are the individual religious identifying with organizations with which they are familiar. Instead these identifications involve a form of religious mapping, whereby respondents indicate their self understood positions vis-à-vis recognized cultural conflicts within the larger religious community.

---

[32] Lindsey, ibid.
[33] Starks, ibid.

Starks' research indicated that traditional and liberal Catholic
movements are loosely rather than tightly linked to the development of
traditional, moderate and liberal Catholic identities. Religious movement
organizations are not socializing agents in the lives of his respondents.
Finally, Starks found that the majority of the Catholic responders in his
research were not members of religious movement organizations and
lacked any direct connection to them.

Starks summarized by stating that religious self -identification as a
traditional or liberal Catholic does not mean one is identifying with a
movement community that directly shapes one's beliefs and actions. Starks
believes that his data is supportive of provides the generalized cultural
conflict model which posits that these self identifications are a form of
mapping, whereby respondents indicated their self understood positions
vis-à-vis recognized cultural conflicts within the larger community.
Furthermore, that Catholic religious divisions are not linear and reducible
to a political stance because religious divisions do not correlate well with
the political divisions of right and left. I interpret Starks conclusions that
in reality other sub cultural identities either in lieu of or in addition to
religious subcultural identities impact not only political attitudes but
identity formation.

Section 4:
Syntheses

*In Two Approaches to Religion and Politics: Moral Cosmology and
Subcultural Identity,* Starks and Robinson (2009)[34] explored the two
competing approaches to internal religious divisions and their political
consequences. The moral cosmology approach as we have seen focuses on
religious worldviews. The subcultural identity approach focuses upon
identity rather than worldview. Specifically in this research study
subcultural identity referred to self- identified Evangelicals and
Fundamentalists who the author expected to be more politically
conservative on both cultural and economic issues when compared to
Mainline or Liberal Protestants.

To investigate similarities and differences between moral cosmology
and religious subcultural identity, data from the 1998 General Social
Survey conducted by the National Opinion Research Center of the

---

[34] Starks, Brian and Robinson, Robert (2009). Two approaches to religion and
politics: Moral cosmology and subcultural identity, *Journal for the Scientific Study
of Religion,* 48 (4)650-669.

University of Chicago was utilized. A three item index was created to measure religious orthodoxy – theological modernism.

The first item in the moral cosmology index measured the belief in divine inspiration and the literal truth of the Bible. In agreeing that the Bible is inerrant, respondents prioritize divine revelation and limited individual interpretive authority. The opposite is true when respondents claimed that the Bible is a book of fables and moral tales. The second item: "I believe in a God who watches over me" measured whether respondents see themselves as affected by and perhaps held accountable to God in their day-to-day lives. The third item: "follow faithfully the teachings of their church or synagogue" captured adherence to theological doctrine rather than the more individualized and contextualized use of religious/moral precepts that characterizes theological modernists. The dependent variables in this study examined two separate policy domains, culture and economics.

Analysis revealed that moral cosmology and subcultural identity are empirically related but not substitutable. Self- identified Evangelicals and Fundamentalists are more orthodox in their moral cosmology then Mainline or Liberal Protestants. Traditional Catholics are more orthodox than moderate or liberal Catholics. Nonetheless differences in orthodoxy between Protestants and Catholics regardless of their sub-cultural identity are considerably larger than those differences between sub-cultural identities within Protestantism and Catholicism. The authors suggested that based upon these finding, subcultural divisions within faith traditions have not supplanted differences between faith traditions at least in terms of moral cosmology.

In conclusion, Starks and Robinson (2009) posit that moral cosmology and subcultural identity are associated but have independent and sometimes opposite effects on the political beliefs and attitudes of Americans. For cultural issues, religious tradition identity and moral cosmology have parallel effects that serve to reinforce or increase overall religious group differences in attitudes toward social cultural issues. Here I suggest that the orthodox subcultural identity is most salient and augmented by religious (tradition) reference group orientation. The Opposite effects were found for moral cosmology and subcultural identity in the domain of economic policy. Here it was demonstrated that the two religious dimensions act as countervailing forces that reduce overall differences between religious groups on economic issues. I further suggest that for economic issues the countervailing effect noted by Starks is attributable to alternative subcultural identities intersecting with religious tradition identity and more salient in motivation and justification for individual action. Religion matters in the formation of identity (Berger 1967)[35] and in the immigrant's adaptation to a new host society (Min 2010).[36] Classical sociology (Weber 1958)[37] makes the case that our religious worldview motivates us and gives justification to our actions. The theory of moral cosmology according to Stark and Robinson (2009) continues in this Weberian fashion and attributes identity formation to religious orthodoxy. Specifically, a high degree of religious orthodoxy will lead an individual towards a communitarian stance on economic issues and an authoritarian stance on social- cultural issues. The nonreligious or the non-orthodox religious are seen as modernists by these authors and are perceived as taking stances that are more individualistic on economic issues and moderate/liberal on issues of social-cultural concern.

---

[35] Berger, ibid.
[36] Min, ibid.
[37] Weber, ibid.

CHAPTER SEVEN

RESULTS:
COMPARISON BETWEEN IMMIGRANT GENERATIONAL STAGE FOR THE EFFECT OF RELIGIOUS ORTHODOXY UPON ECONOMIC AND SOCIAL ISSUES

Chapter Overview

The results section is separated into three chapters: immigrant generational stage (Chapter 7), immigrant generational stage by religious tradition (Chapter 8) and finally immigrant generational stage by gender (Chapter 9). Statistically I have utilized ANOVA and the post hoc test least significant difference (LSD) to capture statistically significant relationships or comparisons between the groups of interest. Individual indices for the dependent variables (religious orthodoxy, economic and social issues) have been computed and the Pearson Rho test has been applied to identify significant correlational relationship between the dependent variables. From a methodological and analytic perspective there are several points of concern that are a result of relying upon the GSS as our data source.

1. Despite the fact that there are some 1652 (25%) non -Christian respondents in our sample, the majority of respondents were Christian. This may skew our data in ways that cannot be predicted. Therefore I believe the data has greater validity if applied primarily to the Christian immigrant population.

2. In order to maintain healthy cell size for statistical analysis, I was unable to capture separately the responses for the non-Christian post 1965 immigrant groups. This is clearly a knowledge gap that needs to be addressed in the future.

3. Again in order to maintain healthy cell size for statistical analysis I was unable to separate protestant tradition by denomination or

religious family (evangelical from moderates) and traditional catholic respondents from moderate catholic respondents. This additional level of analysis is warranted to assure that the data is not skewed in either a moderating or conservative direction.

On a positive note, it is clear that combining the three core components of biblical literalism, practice and subjective sense of religiosity into the aggregate measure of religiosity is design strength. They appear to measure different components of religious orthodoxy and taken together they tell a more complete story.

Comparison between Immigrant Generational Stage for the Effect of Religious Orthodoxy upon Economic and Social Issues

As can be interpreted from the main groups demographic profile (appendix E.1), the research sample was comprised of 6567 individuals that responded to all selected questions administered by the General Social Survey addressing religious orthodoxy and positions on social and economic issues for the 2006, 2008, and 2010 GSS waves. As would be expected the 1.5 generation was the youngest group studied with more than one- half of the respondents being under thirty five years of age (51%). They tended to be single (37.8%) and slightly better educated than the immigrant group (78% of the 1.5 generation completing high school in comparison to 65% in the immigrant group). 86% of the reference group completed high school. Again as would be expected the 2.0 generation and reference group were the better educated. 57% of the 2.0 generation and reference group having attended some college in comparison to immigrant (48%) and 1.5 (51%). Of interest is the fact that the immigrant group had the highest percentage of respondents who attended at least one year of post college education (16%) and more immigrant respondents were married (57%) than any other group.

Relig3

ANOVA (a one way analysis of variance) indicated the presence of unequal means (significant differences) between immigrant generational stages for relig3 (.026), the aggregate mean indices score. Relig3 is comprised of the three core components used to measure religious orthodoxy; biblical literalism (biblit3), practice (pract3) and subjective sense of religiosity (subj3). ANOVA analysis indicated the presence of variability between immigrant generational stages for biblical literalism (>.001), and subjective sense of religiosity (>.002), but not for our measure of religious practice between immigrant generational stages (.158). See table 7.1

Table 7.1: ANOVA

		Sum of Squares	df	Mean Square	F	Sig.
Biblit3	Between Groups	6.890	3	2.297	10.201	**.000
	Within Groups	1473.055	6543	.225		
	Total	1479.945	6546			
Pract3	Between Groups	3.551	3	1.184	1.733	.158
	Within Groups	4473.719	6551	.683		
	Total	4477.270	6554			
Subj3	Between Groups	6.998	3	2.333	4.972	.002
	Within Groups	3074.072	6552	.469		
	Total	3081.071	6555			
religos3	Between Groups	1.414	3	.471	3.097	.026
	Within Groups	998.265	6559	.152		
	Total	999.678	6562			
econ3	Between Groups	83.294	3	27.765	28.119	**.000
	Within Groups	4315.899	4371	.987		
	Total	4399.193	4374			
soc7	Between Groups	.967	3	.322	1.640	.178
	Within Groups	1289.477	6559	.197		
	Total	1290.444	6562			

** = >.001 level

The Fisher least significant difference procedure (LSD), a post hoc test, was used to further analyze the between group (immigrant generational stages) data. On the aggregate measure of religious orthodoxy (relig3), no significant differences were found to be present between the immigrant generation, and the 1.5, 2.0 generations, or reference group. A significant difference was found between the 2.0 generation and reference group (.006) such that the 2.0 generation was statistically more religious orthodox than the reference group as measured by relig3.

When the core components of the measure of religious orthodoxy were analyzed separately (Fisher analysis), significant differences (variability) between immigrant generational stages were found. On the indices of biblical literalism (biblit3), no significant difference was found to exist between the immigrant generation and the 1.5 or 2.0 generations. A significant difference was found between the immigrant generation and the reference group (>.001) with the immigrant generation being more literal

in biblical interpretation then the reference group. The immigrant
generation was the most literal in biblical interpretation of all groups. A
significant difference was also found between the 2.0 generation and the
reference group (.011) such that the 2.0 generation was more literal in
biblical interpretation than the reference group and second only to the
immigrant respondents on this indices.

In the analysis of the responders' subjective sense of religiosity, subj3,
no significant differences were found between the immigrant generation
and the 1.5, 2.0, or reference group. A significant difference was found
between the 2.0 generation and the reference group with the 2.0 generation
having a greater subject sense of religiosity than the reference group. The
2.0 generation had the strongest subject sense of religiosity of all groups.

Finally in our analysis of the data measuring religious practice, pract3,
no significant differences were found between the immigrant generation
and the 1.5, 2.0, or reference group. A significant difference was found
between the 1.5 generation and reference group (>.039), with the 1.5
generation proving to be less active in their religious practice then the
reference group. No significant differences were found between the 1.5
generation and the 2.0 generation or between the 2.0 generation and
reference group for religious practice. See Appendix C.1 for indices scores
for immigrant generational stages.

Religious orthodoxy Summary

- Little variability in religious orthodoxy (as measured by relig3, biblit3,
  subj3 and pract3) was found between immigrant generational stages.
- When variability was indicated it was found between the immigrant
  and 2.0 generation and the reference group on biblical literalism
  (biblit3) and between the 2.0 generation and reference group for the
  aggregate indices (relig3) and (subj3).

Economic Issues

Based upon our data showing little variability in religious orthodoxy
(relig3) between immigrant generational stages and secondly the world
view paradigm of moral cosmology as the primary explanatory theory we
would expect:

1. Little variability between the immigrant generation, the 1.5, 2.0, or
   reference group on the indices of economic issues. This indices can
   be interpreted as a measure of communitarianism – individualism;

the degree to which a respondent views economic responsibility residing within the community and larger institutional structures (government) rather than within the individual.

Summary

Our data is not supportive of the above expected findings.

1. ANOVA analysis indicated significant differences between immigrant generational stages on economic issues (>.001). Although no significant difference was found between the immigrant and 1.5 generation, the Fisher post hoc analysis (LSD) indicated significant differences between the immigrant and 2.0 generation (>.001) and the immigrant generation and reference group (>.001).In both instances the immigrant generation was more communitarian than the comparison group.
2. Fisher post hoc analysis indicated no significant difference between the 2.0 generation and reference group. However significant differences were found between the 2.0 generation and immigrant generation (>.001), the 2.0 generation and the 1.5 generation (.007); significance was found between the reference group and immigrant generation (>.001) and the reference group and 1.5 generation (>.001). The 2.0 and reference group were significantly more individualistic (less communitarian) than both the immigrant and 1.5 generation. In fact individualism increased from the immigrant generation to the second generation with the reference group being the most individualistic (least communitarian) of all.

Again based upon our data and the world view paradigm of moral cosmology as the primary explanatory theory we would expect:

1. Little variability between the immigrant generation, the 1.5, 2.0, or reference group in response to social issues. The indices of social issues (soc7) can be interpreted as a measure of authoritarianism – modernism: the degree to which a respondent views decisions made about social issues residing within the precepts of a religious tradition rather than within the individual.

Table 7.2: ANOVA

		Sum of Squares	df	Mean Square	F	Sig.
Abortion If Woman Wants For Any Reason	Between Groups	5.905	3	1.968	8.133	.000
	Within Groups	1001.008	4136	.242		
	Total	1006.913	4139			
Divorce Laws	Between Groups	5.948	3	1.983	3.684	.012
	Within Groups	2271.216	4220	.538		
	Total	2277.165	4223			
Sex With Person Other Than Spouse	Between Groups	4.706	3	1.569	3.635	.012
	Within Groups	1826.724	4232	.432		
	Total	1831.430	4235			
Feelings About Pornography Laws	Between Groups	2.910	3	.970	3.311	.019
	Within Groups	1277.168	4360	.293		
	Total	1280.078	4363			
Homosexual Sex Relations	Between Groups	83.294	3	27.765	28.119	**.000
	Within Groups	4315.899	4371	.987		
	Total	8048.080	4081			
Homosexuals Should Have Right To Marry	Between Groups	59.539	3	19.846	8.723	.000
	Within Groups	9655.455	4244	2.275		
	Total	9714.993	4247			
Sex Before Marriage	Between Groups	16.880	3	5.627	3.643	.012
	Within Groups	6676.257	4323	1.544		
	Total	6693.137	4326			

Social Issues

Again based upon our data and the world view paradigm of moral cosmology as the primary explanatory theory we would expect:

1. Little variability between the immigrant generation, the 1.5, 2.0, or reference group in response to social issues. The indices of social issues (soc7) can be interpreted as a measure of authoritarianism – modernism: the degree to which a respondent views decisions made about social issues residing within the precepts of a religious tradition rather than within the individual.

Summary

Our data is partially supportive to the above expectations for responses to social issues.

ANOVA analysis indicated no significant difference between the immigrant generational stages for the mean aggregate scale score for all seven questions addressing social issues, soc7 (.178) See table 7.1. However the bye question analysis (ANOVA) of the seven questions comprising soc7 indicated significant differences between immigrant generational stages for all seven questions. See table 7.2. Further analysis using the Fisher post hoc test (LSD), indicated which of the comparisons between the immigrant generational stages were significant.

- On the issue of abortion, significant differences (LSD) were found between the immigrant generation and the 1.5 generation(.024), the 2.0 generation(.001) and the reference group(>.001) . In all of these comparisons the immigrant generation was the more authoritarian.
- On the issue of divorce, significant differences were found between the immigrant generation and reference group (.031) and the 2.0 generation and the reference group (.038). In both of these comparisons the reference group was found to be the more authoritarian.
- On the question addressing sex with a person other than spouse, significant differences were found between the 1.5 generation and the second generation (.047) and the 1.5 generation and the reference group (.002). Here the 1.5 generation was more authoritarian than all other comparison group.
- On the issue of pornography significant differences were found between the immigrant and 1.5 generation (.01), and the immigrant and the 2.0 generation (.013) and the immigrant and reference group (.037). Here the immigrant generation was the least authoritarian in all comparisons.
- On the issue of homosexual sex relationship, significant differences were obtained for the immigrant generation and the 1.5 generation (>.001), the immigrant generation and the 2.0 generation (>.001) and the immigrant generation and the reference group (>.001). Here the immigrant generation was the least authoritarian. The second generation was more authoritarian than all other groups on this question.
- In addressing the issue of homosexuals having the right to marry, significant differences were found between the immigrant generation and the 1.5 generation(.019), the immigrant generation and the 2.0 generation(>.001), the immigrant generation and reference group(>.001) with the immigrant generation being once again the most authoritarian.
- Lastly with our question addressing sex before marriage, significant differences were obtained between the immigrant generation and

1.5 generation (.012), and the immigrant generation and 2.0 generation (.007). Here the immigrant generation was least authoritarian. The 2.0 generation was found to be significantly different from the reference group and more authoritarian (.044).

Pearson Rho statistical analysis was used to test for significant correlations between religious orthodoxy and stances on issues of economic and social concerns. Rho correlations indicated the absence of significance between the aggregate measure (relig3) or any of the core components and the stances on economic (econ3) or social (soc7) issues for all immigrant generational stages. See appendix D.1.

CHAPTER EIGHT

RESULTS: COMPARISON BETWEEN RELIGIOUS TRADITIONS (CATHOLIC/PROTESTANT) FOR THE COMBINED EFFECT OF RELIGIOUS ORTHODOXY AND IMMIGRANT GENERATIONAL STAGE UPON ECONOMIC AND SOCIAL ISSUES

As can be interpreted from the main groups by religious tradition demographic profile (appendix E.2) the Catholic cohort is slightly older than the Protestant cohort (28% vs. 20.6% under the age of 35); the exception being the 1.5 generation. Here 52% of the Catholics in this generation were under 35 years of age in comparison to 21% in the Protestant 1.5 generation. The Catholic 1.5 generation was the youngest generation of all groups (religious traditions) studied. There was little difference between religious traditions for educational attainment or marital status. It should be noted that for the comparisons made between Catholics and Protestants, a subset of the reference group was utilized consisting of only the Catholic and Protestant respondents.

Relig3

Unequal means (SD) (Anova) for the dependent variable Relig3, the aggregate mean scale score for religious orthodoxy was found across religious traditions (.>001) but not within religious traditions between immigrant generational stages(.133) . When analyzing within religious traditions between immigrant generational stages no comparisons were found to be significant for the catholic cohort. Significant differences were found within the protestant cohort; specifically between the protestant immigrants and the protestant 1.5 generation (Pi-P1.5) with the Protestant immigrant generational stage being more religious orthodox (.05). A significant difference was also found for the comparison between the

Protestant 1.5 and 2.0 generations. Here the Protestant 2.0 generation was significantly more religiously orthodox (.05),

When analyzing relig3 across religious traditions, significant difference was found for the comparison between the Catholic and Protestant reference groups (Cr-Pr) and between the Catholic and Protestant 1.5 generation (C1.5-P1.5) with the Catholics being more religiously orthodox as measured by our aggregate mean scale score for religious orthodoxy in both comparisons (.05). However as can be seen in the plot for relig3 by religious tradition, Catholics were more religiously orthodox than Protestants in all comparisons for this measure. See table 8.1 for Anova test of significance for relig3 by religious tradition, Appendix C.2 for indices scores of religious orthodoxy by the intersection of immigrant generational stage and religious tradition.

When the core components of our measure of religious orthodoxy were analyzed separately (ANOVA) across religious traditions, significant differences were found for all three components: biblit3, subj3, and pract3; (>.001). When the core components of our measure of religious orthodoxy were analyzed separately within religious traditions and between immigrant generational stages, significant differences were found for biblit3 (.001), and pract3 (.001) but not for sub3 (.745). See tables 8.2, 8.3 and 8.4.

The within religious tradition analysis of biblit3 between immigrant generational stages, found significant difference for comparisons made between the Catholic immigrants and the Catholic reference group (Ci-Cr) with the Catholic immigrants being more literal in their biblical interpretation(.05). No other significant comparison was observed within either the Catholic or Protestant traditions between immigrant generational stages for this measure. In the analysis across religious traditions for biblit3, significant comparisons were found between the immigrant generations (Ci-Pi) and the 1.5 generation (C1.5-P1.5) with the Catholics being more literal in biblical interpretation than the Protestants in both comparisons (.05). See Plot 8.2 for biblit3 by religious tradition.

In our analysis of subj3, no significant differences were found for either Catholics or Protestants between immigrant generational stages within their specific religious tradition. In our analysis across religious traditions, significant differences were found for the comparisons between the immigrant, 1.5 generation, and the reference groups (Ci-Pi; C1.5-P1.5: Cr-Pr), with Catholics having a stronger sense of subjective religiosity in all comparisons. See plot 8.3 for subj3 by religious tradition.

Finally in our analysis of the data measuring religious practice, pract3, significant differences were obtained both across religious traditions (.001)

and within religious tradition between immigrant generational stages (.001). In the within religious tradition analysis for the Catholic cohort no significant differences between immigrant generational stages were obtained. Significant differences were found for comparisons within the Protestant tradition between immigrant generational stages; specifically between the Protestant immigrants and 1.5 generation (Pi-P1.5) and again between the Protestant immigrant and their reference group (Pi-Pr) with the Protestant immigrants having a more active religious life in both comparisons (.05). In the across religious tradition analysis we again found Protestant immigrants having a more active religious life than Catholic immigrants (Ci-Pi) (.05). In fact the Protestant immigrant religious life was more active than the religious life for all Catholic immigrant generational stages. See plot 8.4.

Religious Orthodoxy Summary

- Little variability in religious orthodoxy (as measured by relig3, our aggregate mean scale score) was found within religious traditions between immigrant generation stages. Although in two of the three core components of relig3 (biblit3 and pract3) we did find significant differences for some comparisons within the religious tradition. Specifically, Catholic immigrants were more literal in biblical interpretation (than other Catholic immigrant generational stages) and protestant immigrants more active in religious life (than other Protestant immigrant generational stages).

- Greater variability in religious orthodoxy was found across religious traditions. Catholic immigrants were the most literal in their interpretation of the Bible, more so than any other Catholic comparison and all Protestant groups. Catholics in all immigrant generational stages had a stronger sense of subjective religiosity than Protestants. However, Protestants had a more active religious life that all comparable Catholic groups.

Economic Issues

Based upon our data showing little variability in religious orthodoxy within each religious tradition and greater variability across religious traditions, and the worldview paradigm of moral cosmology as the primary explanatory theory, we would expect:

1. Little variability in response to economic issues within each religious tradition.
2. Greater variability across religious traditions in response to economic issues. We would expect that Catholics, being more religiously orthodox (relig3), would be more communitarian on economic issues than Protestants.

Summary

Our data is not supportive of the above expected findings.

- No significant differences were found across religious traditions for economic issues for any comparisons.
- Within religious tradition analysis we found significant differences between immigrant generational stages (.04). Within the Catholic tradition (economic issues), significant differences were obtained for comparisons between the immigrant and 2.0 generation (Ci-C2.0)), the immigrant and the reference group (Ci-Cr), and for the 1.5 generation and reference group (C1.5-Cr) (.05). Within the Protestant tradition, significant differences were found for comparisons between the immigrant generational stages for the immigrant and reference group (Pi-Pr) and for the 1.5 generation and reference group (P1.5-Pr) (.05). In all of these comparisons, the immigrant and 1.5 generation are more communitarian in their approach to economic issues then either the 2.0 generation or reference group, irrespective of religious tradition. See table 8.5 and plot 8.5.

Social Issues

Again based upon our data, and the world view paradigm of moral cosmology as the primary explanatory theory, we would expect:

1. Little variability within religious tradition in response to social issues within each of the religious traditions. Given that the Catholic immigrant generation demonstrated greater religious orthodoxy as measured in two of the three core components of relig3 (biblit3 and subj3), we expect that the catholic immigrant generation will demonstrate a more authoritarian stance on social issues than all other Catholic immigrant generational stages. In addition, given that the Protestant immigrant generation

demonstrated greater religious orthodoxy as measured by relig3 and pract3, we expect that the Protestant immigrant generation will demonstrate a more authoritarian stance on social issues than all other protestant immigrant generations.

2. Greater variability across religious traditions. We would expect that Catholics being more religiously orthodox (measured by relig3), and more literal in biblical interpretation, would be more authoritarian on social issues than the Protestant cohort.

Summary

Our data is partially supportive of the above expectations for responses to social issues.

- We observed significant differences both across religious traditions (>.001) and within religious traditions between immigrant generational stages (.>001), on the aggregate mean scale score for all social issues (Soc7). Specifically for Soc7 within the Catholic tradition, comparison analysis showed that the Catholic reference group was significantly (.05) more authoritarian than either the Catholic immigrant or Catholic 2.0 generation and most authoritarian of all Catholics immigrant generational stages. No significant comparisons were observed within the Protestant tradition between immigrant generational stages for Soc7 or any of the seven questions comprising this scale. In the analysis across religious traditions for the aggregate mean scale score for social issues (Soc7), only the reference groups were significantly different (Cr-Pr) with Catholics being more authoritarian than Protestants (.05). See table 8.6 and plot 8.6 for visual presentation of soc7 data.

In a bye question analysis of the items comprising soc7, significant comparisons were found across religious traditions for all seven questions comprising our scale for social issues; abortion (.029), divorce (.012), sex with another partner (.003), pornography (>.001), homosexual sex relationships (>.001), homosexual marriage (>.001), sex before marriage (>.001). In the across religious tradition analysis, Protestants were more authoritarian than Catholics on the question addressing divorce and a homosexual's right to marry. Catholics were more authoritarian than Protestants on questions addressing: sex with another person beside your spouse, pornography, homosexual relations and sex before marriage.

Analysis of comparisons within religious traditions and between immigrant generational stages found significant differences for four questions: abortion (.015), divorce (.001), homosexual relationship (>.001), and sex before marriage (.024).

1. On the question addressing Divorce significant differences were found both across (.012) and within religious traditions between immigrant generational stages (.001).Significant differences were found for comparisons between the catholic and protestant immigrant generations (Ci-Pi) and between the catholic and protestant 1.5 generation (C1.5-P1.5) with Protestants significantly more authoritarian in both comparisons (.05). In fact Protestants were more authoritarian than Catholics on this issue in all comparisons. Within religious tradition for this question found no significant differences within the Protestant cohort. However for Catholics, a significant difference was found for the comparison between Catholic immigrants and Catholic reference group (Ci-Cr), with the Catholic reference group more authoritarian on this question. In fact the Catholic reference group was the most authoritarian on this question of all Catholic immigrant generational stages. See table 8.7 and plot 8.7 for visual presentation of data.

2. On the issue of homosexual marriage, significant differences were found only across religious traditions (>.001), with Protestants more authoritarian than Catholics in all comparisons. However, only the comparison between the Catholic and Protestant reference group (Cr-Pr) and the Catholic and protestant immigrant generation (Ci-Pi) were significantly different on this question (.05). The within religious tradition analysis did find a significant comparison between the catholic immigrant generation and reference group (Ci-Cr) with the Catholic immigrant generation being more authoritarian (.05). See table 8.8 and plot 8.8.

3. On the question of sex with another person other than spouse, a significant difference was found across religious traditions (.003). Specifically for the comparison between the Catholic and protestant 1.5 generation (C1.5-P1.5) with Catholics being the more authoritarian. No comparisons were found to be significant within religious tradition between immigrant generational stages. See table 8.11 and plot 8.11.

4. On the question addressing pornography, significant differences were found across religious traditions (>.001) and for the comparisons between Catholic 2.0 and Protestant 2.0 generation

(C2-P2) and the Catholic and Protestant reference groups (Cr-Pr) with Catholics being more authoritarian (.05). Within religious tradition analysis between immigrant generational stages found significant differences for the comparisons between Catholic immigrant generation and Catholic reference group (Ci-Cr) and the Catholic immigrant generation and Catholic 1.5 generation (Ci-C1.5) with the catholic immigrant generation less authoritarian in both comparisons (.05). See table 8.9 and plot 8.9.

5. On the issue of homosexual sex relations significant differences were found both across (>.001) and within religious traditions (>.001). In across religious tradition analysis the comparisons between Catholic and Protestant reference groups (Cr-Pr), was found significant with the Catholic reference group more authoritarian on this issue (.05). However, Catholics were more authoritarian than Protestant in all comparisons. The within religious tradition analysis for the Catholic cohort found significant differences for the comparisons between the catholic immigrant and Catholic 1.5 generation (Ci-C1.5), the Catholic immigrant and Catholic 2.0 generation (Ci-C2.0) and the Catholic immigrant and the Catholic reference group (Ci-Cr). In all of these comparisons the Catholic immigrant generation was significantly less authoritarian (.05). See table 8.10 and plot 8.10.

6. On the issue of sex before marriage significant differences were found across religious traditions (>.001). In the across religious religion analysis, the comparisons between the Catholic and Protestant reference groups (Cr-Pr) and the Catholic and Protestant immigrant generations (Ci-Pi) was found to be significant with Catholics more authoritarian in both comparisons (.05). In fact Catholics were more authoritarian than Protestants in all comparisons except for the comparison between the Catholic and Protestant 2.0 generation (C2.0-P2.0) where protestant were more authoritarian. The within religious tradition analysis found no comparisons to be significant. See table 8.12 and plot 8.12.

7. Lastly on the issue of abortion, significant differences were found within religious tradition analysis between immigrant generational stages (.015) but not across religious traditions. The within religious tradition analysis between immigrant generational stages found significant differences for the comparisons between the Catholic immigrant and Catholic 1.5 generation (CI-C1.5), the Catholic immigrant and Catholic 2.0 (Ci-C2.0) and the Catholic immigrant and Catholic reference group (CI-Cr) with the Catholic

immigrant generation more authoritarian in all comparisons (.05).the comparison between the catholic and Protestant reference group was found to be significantly different (Cr-Pr) with Catholics more authoritarian. In other comparison, Catholic and Protestant immigrant and 2.0 generations (Ci-Pi; C2.0-P2.0), Catholics again were found to be more authoritarian but not at significant level. Only in the comparison between Catholic 1.5 and Protestant1.5 (C1.5-P1.5) were Protestants more authoritarian on this issue of abortion than Catholics but again not a significant level. See table 8.13 and plot 8.13.

Table 8.1: Tests of Between-Subjects Effects
Dependent Variable: Index relig3

Source	Type I Sum of Squares	df	Mean Square	F	Sig.	Partial Eta Squared
Corrected Model	6.239[a]	7	.891	8.401	.000	.012
Intercept	27856.401	1	27856.401	262580.103	.000	.982
Cathprot	3.856	1	3.856	36.347	**.000	.007
IGS * Cathprot	.594	3	.198	1.865	.133	.001
Error	520.570	4907	.106			
Total	28383.210	4915				
Corrected Total	526.809	4914				

a. R Squared = .012 (Adjusted R Squared = .010)
** = >.001 level

Plot 8.1: Relig3 by religious tradition

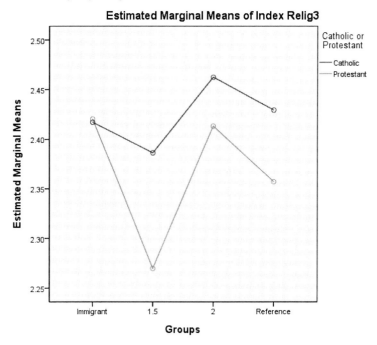

Table 8.2: Tests of Between-Subjects Effects
Dependent Variable: Index bibLit

Source	Type I Sum of Squares	df	Mean Square	F	Sig.	Partial Eta Squared
Corrected Model	12.386^a	7	1.769	10.241	.000	.014
Intercept	39759.968	1	39759.968	230123.401	.000	.979
Cathprot	4.337	1	4.337	25.104	**.000	.005
IGS * Cathprot	2.896	3	.965	5.586	.001	.003
Error	846.952	4902	.173			
Total	40619.306	4910				
Corrected Total	859.338	4909				

a. R Squared = .014 (Adjusted R Squared = .013)
** = >.001 level

Plot 8.2: Biblit3 by religious tradition

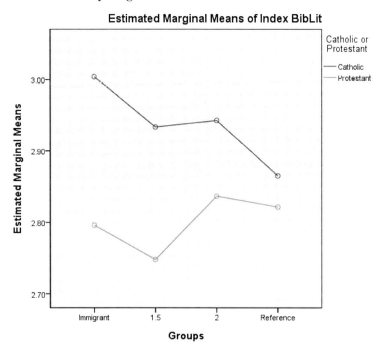

Estimated Marginal Means of Index BibLit

Table 8.3: Tests of Between-Subjects Effects

Dependent Variable: Index Subj3 by religious tradition

Source	Type I Sum of Squares	df	Mean Square	F	Sig.	Partial Eta Squared
Corrected Model	52.939[a]	7	7.563	33.755	.000	.046
Intercept	15162.663	1	15162.663	67676.046	.000	.932
Cathprot	43.824	1	43.824	195.603	**.000	.038
IGS * Cathprot	.276	3	.092	.411	.745	.000
Error	1098.954	4905	.224			
Total	16314.556	4913				
Corrected Total	1151.893	4912				

a. R Squared = .046 (Adjusted R Squared = .045)

** = >.001 level

Plot 8.3: Subj3 by religious tradition

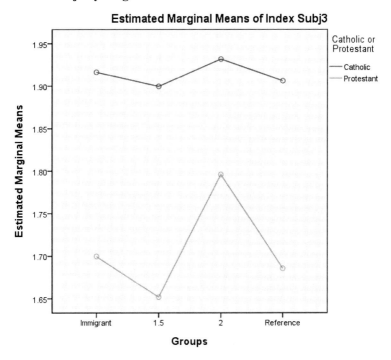

Table 8.4: Tests of Between-Subjects Effects
Dependent Variable: Index pract3 by religious tradition

Source	Type I Sum of Squares	df	Mean Square	F	Sig.	Partial Eta Squared
Corrected Model	22.121[a]	7	3.160	5.075	.000	.007
Intercept	32260.167	1	32260.167	51809.419	.000	.914
Cathprot	6.544	1	6.544	10.509	.001	.002
IGS * Cathprot	10.122	3	3.374	5.419	.001	.003
Error	3053.573	4904	.623			
Total	35335.861	4912				
Corrected Total	3075.694	4911				

a. R Squared = .007 (Adjusted R Squared = .006)

Plot 8.4: Pract3 by religious tradition

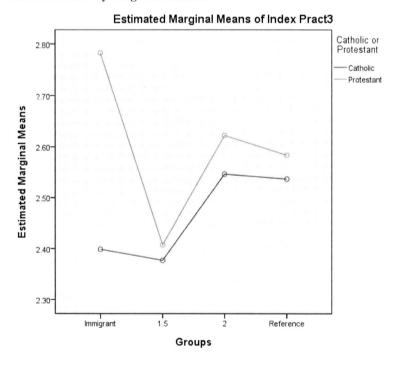

Table 8.5: Tests of Between-Subjects Effects
Dependent Variable: Index econ3 by religious tradition

Source	Type I Sum of Squares	df	Mean Square	F	Sig.	Partial Eta Squared
Corrected Model	85.485[a]	7	12.212	12.274	.000	.025
Intercept	25891.633	1	25891.633	26022.098	.000	.888
Cathprot	4.204	1	4.204	4.226	..665	.001
IGS * Cathprot	1.568	3	.523	.525	..040	.000
Error	3270.520	3287	.995			
Total	29247.639	3295				
Corrected Total	3356.005	3294				

a. R Squared = .025 (Adjusted R Squared = .023)

Plot 8.5: Econ3 by religious tradition

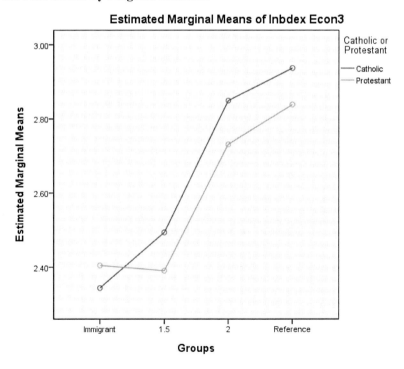

Table 8.6: Tests of Between-Subjects Effects
Dependent Variable: Index Soc7

Source	Type I Sum of Squares	df	Mean Square	F	Sig.	Partial Eta Squared
Corrected Model	16.146[a]	7	2.307	12.262	.000	.017
Intercept	21719.925	1	21719.925	115470.106	.000	.959
Cathprot	11.540	1	11.540	61.349	**.000	.012
IGS * Cathprot	3.741	3	1.247	6.629	**.000	.004
Error	922.254	4903	.188			
Total	22658.325	4911				
Corrected Total	938.400	4910				

a. R Squared = .017 (Adjusted R Squared = .016)
** = >.001 level

Plot 8.6: Soc7 by religious tradition

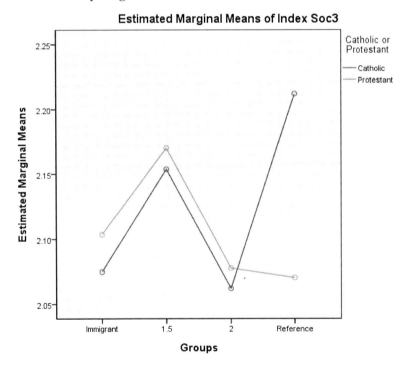

Estimated Marginal Means of Index Soc3

Table 8.7: Tests of Between-Subjects Effects
Dependent Variable: Divorce laws

Source	Type I Sum of Squares	df	Mean Square	F	Sig.	Partial Eta Squared
Corrected Model	20.059[a]	7	2.866	5.816	.000	.013
Intercept	12239.420	1	12239.420	24840.672	.000	.887
Cathprot	3.108	1	3.108	6.308	.012	.002
IGS * Cathprot	7.930	3	2.643	5.365	.001	.005
Error	1554.522	3155	.493			
Total	13814.000	3163				
Corrected Total	1574.580	3162				

R Squared = .013 (Adjusted R Squared = .011)

Plot 8.7: Divorce by religious tradition

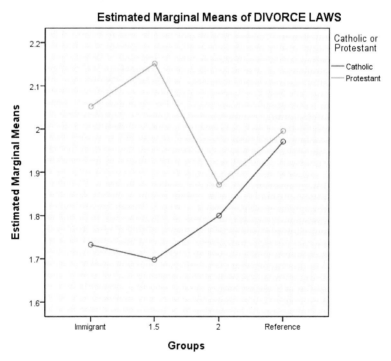

Table 8.8: Tests of Between-Subjects Effects
Dependent Variable: Homosexuals should have right to marry

Source	Type I Sum of Squares	df	Mean Square	F	Sig.	Partial Eta Squared
Corrected Model	237.898[a]	7	33.985	16.361	.000	.035
Intercept	37986.810	1	37986.810	18287.002	.000	.852
Cathprot	197.682	1	197.682	95.165	**.000	.029
IGS * Cathprot	3.918	3	1.306	.629	.596	.001
Error	6595.292	3175	2.077			
Total	44820.000	3183				
Corrected Total	6833.190	3182				

a. R Squared = .035 (Adjusted R Squared = .033)
** = >.001 level

Plot 8.8: Homosexual right to marry

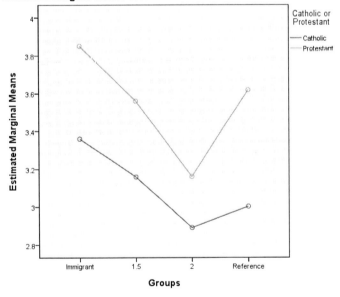

Estimated Marginal Means of HOMOSEXUALS SHOULD HAVE RIGHT TO MARRY

Table 8.9: Tests of Between-Subjects Effects
Dependent Variable: Feelings about pornography laws

Source	Type I Sum of Squares	df	Mean Square	F	Sig.	Partial Eta Squared
Corrected Model	16.308[a]	7	2.330	7.947	.000	.017
Intercept	8580.055	1	8580.055	29268.957	.000	.899
Cathprot	11.008	1	11.008	37.553	**.000	.011
IGS * Cathprot	1.857	3	.619	2.111	.097	.002
Error	960.637	3277	.293			
Total	9557.000	3285				
Corrected Total	976.945	3284				

a. R Squared = .017 (Adjusted R Squared = .015)
** = >.001 level

Plot 8.9: Pornography by religious tradition

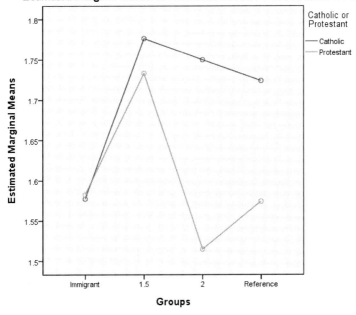

Table 8.10: Tests of Between-Subjects Effects
Dependent Variable: Homosexual sex relations

Source	Type I Sum of Squares	df	Mean Square	F	Sig.	Partial Eta Squared
Corrected Model	259.981[a]	7	37.140	21.409	.000	.047
Intercept	12941.665	1	12941.665	7460.018	.000	.710
Cathprot	195.866	1	195.866	112.904	**.000	.036
IGS * Cathprot	31.560	3	10.520	6.064	**.000	.006
Error	5296.355	3053	1.735			
Total	18498.000	3061				
Corrected Total	5556.335	3060				

a. R Squared = .047 (Adjusted R Squared = .045)
** = >.001 level

Plot 8.10: Homosexual sex relations by religious tradition

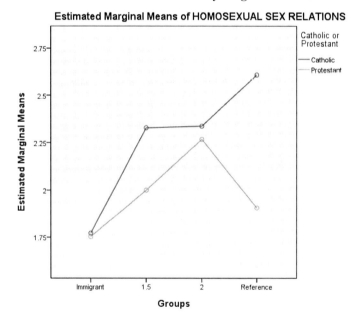

Table 8.11: Tests of Between-Subjects Effects
Dependent Variable: Sex with person other than spouse

Source	Type I Sum of Squares	df	Mean Square	F	Sig.	Partial Eta Squared
Corrected Model	8.461[a]	7	1.209	3.601	.001	.008
Intercept	4811.368	1	4811.368	14332.514	.000	.819
Cathprot	3.011	1	3.011	8.969	.003	.003
IGS * Cathprot	2.034	3	.678	2.020	.109	.002
Error	1066.171	3176	.336			
Total	5886.000	3184				
Corrected Total	1074.632	3183				

a. R Squared = .008 (Adjusted R Squared = .006)

Plot 8.11: Sex with another person

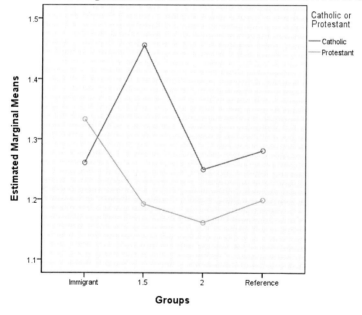

Estimated Marginal Means of SEX WITH PERSON OTHER THAN SPOUSE

Table 8.12: Tests of Between-Subjects Effects
Dependent Variable: Sex before marriage

Source	Type I Sum of Squares	df	Mean Square	F	Sig.	Partial Eta Squared
Corrected Model	218.964[a]	7	31.281	20.038	.000	.042
Intercept	24551.241	1	24551.241	15727.173	.000	.831
Cathprot	193.492	1	193.492	123.948	**.000	.037
IGS * Cathprot	14.763	3	4.921	3.152	.024	.003
Error	5004.795	3206	1.561			
Total	29775.000	3214				
Corrected Total	5223.759	3213				

a. R Squared = .042 (Adjusted R Squared = .040)
** = >.001 level

Plot 8.12: Sex before marriage

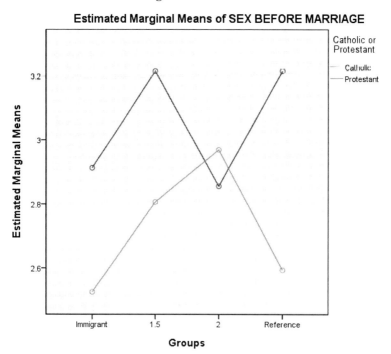

Table 8.13: Tests of Between-Subjects Effects
Dependent Variable: Abortion if woman wants for any reason

Source	Type I Sum of Squares	df	Mean Square	F	Sig.	Partial Eta Squared
Corrected Model	8.855[a]	7	1.265	5.575	.000	.012
Intercept	8384.328	1	8384.328	36950.826	.000	.923
Cathprot	1.078	1	1.078	4.751	.529	.002
IGS * Cathprot	2.366	3	.789	3.475	.015	.003
Error	701.817	3093	.227			
Total	9095.000	3101				
Corrected Total	710.672	3100				

a. R Squared = .012 (Adjusted R Squared = .010)

Plot 8.13: Abortion by religious tradition

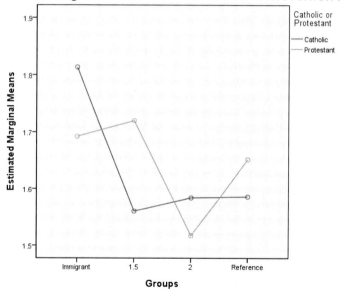

Estimated Marginal Means of ABORTION IF WOMAN WANTS FOR ANY REASON

CHAPTER NINE

RESULTS:
COMPARISON BETWEEN GENDER FOR THE COMBINED EFFECT OF RELIGIOUS ORTHODOXY AND IMMIGRANT GENERATIONAL STAGE UPON ECONOMIC AND SOCIAL ISSUES

As can be interpreted from the main group by gender demographic profiles (appendix E.3) there are more females in the sample (56%) and more present in all of the main groups. Females were slightly older than males; 66% being over the age of thirty-five in comparison to 63%. The two exceptions being the 1.5 generation where males were older (71% over thirty-five compared to 53%), and in the seventy-five plus category where there were more men over seventy five than women (23.6% compared to 5.5%). There was little difference in educational attainment between genders as measured by percent completing high school. Of interest there were more female immigrants (13%) who had some post college education in comparison to men with post college experience (8.6%).

Relig3

Unequal means (SD ANOVA) for the dependent variable relig3, the aggregate mean scale score for religious orthodoxy were found across gender (>.001) but not within gender, between immigrant generational stages (.486). When analyzing across gender for relig3, some comparisons were found to be significant (Fisher LSD). Specifically significant differences were obtained between male immigrants and female immigrants (Mi-Fi) as well as between the male and female reference groups (Mr-Fr) (.05). In both of these comparisons males were more religiously orthodox than the females. In fact males were more religiously orthodox as measured by relig3 in all comparison to the female cohort.

When analyzing within gender and between immigrant generational stages, no comparisons were found to be significant within the male cohort and between immigrant generational stages on relig3. Within the female cohort some comparisons proved significant. A significant difference was found between the female second generation and female reference group (F2-Fr), with the female second-generation being statistically more religiously orthodox than the reference group (.05) and more religious orthodox than all other female groups. See table 9.1 and plot 9.1 for relig3 by gender.

When the core components of our measure of religious orthodoxy were analyzed separately (Anova) for across religious traditions, significant differences were found in all three components: biblit3, subj3 and pract3. (>.001). When the three core components of our measure of religious orthodoxy were analyzed separately within gender no significant differences were obtained in either the male or female cohort. See table 9.2, 9.3 and 9.4 for Anova tests of significance, Appendix C.3 for indices scores for religious orthodoxy by intersection of immigrant generational stage and gender.

The within gender analysis of biblit3 between immigrant generational stages, yielded no significant difference for any male comparison. Within the female cohort some comparisons between immigrant generational stages were significant. In the comparison between the female immigrants and female reference group (Fi-Fr), the female immigrant generation proved to be statistically more literal in biblical interpretation (.05). The female immigrant generation along with the female second-generation proved to be the more literal in biblical interpretation of all of the female groups. Across gender analysis for biblit3, showed both the female immigrant and the female second-generation to be more literal in interpretation of the bible than any male group. See plot 9.2 for biblit3 by gender.

In our analysis of subj3, no significant differences were found in the male cohort between immigrant generational stages. Within the female cohort some comparisons were found to be significant; specifically (F2-Fr) (.05); the female second-generation demonstrating the strongest sense of subjective religiosity of all female groups. Across gender analysis demonstrated significant differences for the comparison between the immigrant male and the immigrant female generation (Im-If), as well as between the reference male and reference female group (Rm-Rf). In both comparisons males demonstrated a stronger sense of subjective religiosity than females including the female second-generation (.05). See plot 9.3 for Subj3 by gender.

Finally in our analysis of the data measuring religious practice, pract3, no significant differences were found within the male cohort between immigrant generational stages. However the male second-generation demonstrated the most active religious life of all male groups. Within the female cohort no significant difference was found between immigrant generational stages, however the female second-generation demonstrated the most active religious life of all female groups. In across gender analysis significant differences were noted for the following comparisons: immigrant male and immigrant female (Im-If), the 1.5male and the 1.5 female generation (1.5m -1.5f) and the reference male and reference female group (Rm –Rf). In all of these comparisons males demonstrated a significantly more active religious life (.05). See plot 9.4 for pract3 by gender.

Religious Orthodox Summary

- Little variability in religious orthodoxy (as measured byRelig3, our aggregate means scale score) was found within gender, between immigrant generational stages. This was especially evident in the male cohort, where male religious orthodoxy was stable across immigrant generational stages on all measures (relig3, biblit3, subj3 and pract3).
- Greater variability in religious orthodoxy was found across gender (as measured by relig3), with the male cohort demonstrating greater religious orthodoxy than the female cohort.
- On the issue of biblical literalism, the female immigrant and second generation were more literal in their interpretation of the Bible, then all other female groups and all male groups
- On the issue of subjective religiosity, males in all immigrant generational stages had a stronger sense of subjective religiosity than females
- In the area of religious practice, males had a more active religious life than all comparable female groups.

Economic Issues

Based upon our data showing little variability in religious orthodoxy within gender, and greater variability across gender and the worldview paradigm of moral cosmology as the primary explanatory theory, we would expect:

1. Little variability in response to economic issues within each gender especially in the male cohort. We predict that a male

communitarian economic position is stabile between immigrant generational stages.

2. Significant variability on economic issues across gender. We predict that males, being more religiously orthodox (as measured by relig3), would be more communitarian in their economic position than females.

Summary

Our data is not supportive of the above expected findings for economic issues.

- Our data demonstrated no significant difference across gender (.741) on the economic scale but a significant difference within gender and between immigrant generational stages (.011). Only the comparison between the reference male and reference female generation (Rm –Rf) was found to be significant (.05), with the reference male generation being more individualistic than the reference female generation. Males despite demonstrating a greater degree of religious orthodoxy are more individualistic than females in all comparisons.

- Within gender analysis yielded significant differences for some comparisons between immigrant generational stages. Within the male cohort, significant differences (.05) were obtained between (Mi –M2; Mi – Mr; M1.5 – Mr) with male reference group being the most individualistic in all comparisons and the male immigrant and male 1.5 generation being the most communitarian. Within the female cohort, some comparisons were found to be significant. Specifically, the comparisons between the female immigrant and female 2.0 generation, female immigrant and female reference group and the female 1.5 and female reference group (Fi-F2;Fi-Fr;F1.5-Fr), with the female reference group being the most individualistic in all comparisons and the female immigrant and female 1.5 generation being the most communitarian. See table 9.5 and plot 9.5.

Social Issues

Again based upon our data and the world view paradigm of moral cosmology as the primary explanatory theory, we would expect:

1. Little variability in response to social issues within each gender (as measured by soc7); especially for the male cohort. Given that the female second generation is more religiously orthodox (relig3), more literal in biblical interpretation (biblit3), has a greater subjective sense of religiosity(subj3) and is more active in practice (pract3) than all other female groups, we expect the female second-generation to be the most authoritative of all female immigrant generation stages on social issues.

2. Significant variability on social issues across gender. Given that the male cohort is significantly more religiously orthodox than females (as measured by Relig3) , have a stronger subjective sense of religiosity than the female cohort and are more active in religious life than the females, we would expect the male cohort to be more authoritative in all comparisons to the female cohort on social issues.

Summary

Our data is supportive of the above expected findings for responses to social issues.

- We observed significant differences (>.001) in across gender comparisons on the aggregate mean scale score for all social issues(Soc7), and no significant differences within gender (between immigrant generational stages) on Soc7. However some individual comparisons within gender on Soc7 were significant. Specifically the within gender comparison between male immigrants and male reference group (Mi-Mr) indicated that the male reference group was more authoritative than the male immigrant group (.05). No comparisons were found significant in the female cohort.

- In our across gender analysis for Soc7, we found significant differences only between the male reference group and the female reference group (Mr-Fr) with the male reference group being significantly more authoritative (.05). It is clear from the plot of Soc7 by gender, that males are more authoritative than females in all comparisons as expected. See Table 9.6 and plot 9.6.

In a bye question analysis significant differences were found across gender for only four questions: pornography (>.001), homosexual sex relations (.019), homosexual right to marry (>.001) and sex before marriage (.013). We found no significant differences across gender on the questions addressing abortion, divorce and sex with another person other than spouse.

1. In our comparison across gender for the question addressing pornography, significant differences (.05) were found in all immigrant generational stages with the males more authoritarian than the females in all comparisons. No within gender comparisons were significant. See table 9.7and plot 9.7.

2. For the question addressing homosexual sex relations, we found a significant difference across gender (.05) between the male and female reference groups (Mr-Fr) and between the male2.0 and female 2.0 generation (M2.0-F2.0) with the females being more authoritative in both comparisons. Females were more authoritative in all comparison between genders on this question but not at the significant level of .05. No within gender comparisons were found to be significant. See table 9.8 and plot 9.8.

3. For the question addressing homosexual's right to marry significant difference (.05) was found for the comparisons between the male and female 1.5 generation (M1.5-F1.5) and between the male and female 2.0 generation (M1.5-F1.5) with the males being more authoritarian in both comparisons. Of interest, the female second-generation was the least authoritarian of all groups both male and female on this question. See table 9.9 and plot 9.9.

4. Lastly on the question addressing sex before marriage, a significant difference (.05) was found for the comparison between the male and female reference group (Mr-Fr) with the male reference group being more authoritative. Males were more authoritarian than females on this question in all comparisons, but not at the .05 level of significance. See table 9.10 and plot 9.10.

In the bye question analysis within gender and between immigrant generational stages no significant differences were found in any of our seven questions comprising soc7. However some comparisons were found to be significant.

5. On the question addressing abortion, a significant difference was found between the male immigrant and reference group (Mi-Mr), with the male immigrant generation being significantly more authoritarian than the reference group (.05) and the most authoritarian of all male groups. Within the female cohort, we found a significant difference (.05) between the female immigrant and female reference group (Fi-Fr) with the female immigrant

being significantly more authoritarian than the reference group (.05) and the most authoritarian of all female groups. No significant difference was found across gender for any comparison. See Table 9.11 and plot 9.11.

6. On the question addressing divorce, a significant difference was found in the comparison between the male 1.5 generation and male reference group (M1.5-Mr) with the male reference group significantly more authoritarian (.05). In fact the male reference group was the most authoritarian on this question of all male immigrant generational stages. No comparisons were found to be significant within the female cohort or across gender. See table 9.12 and Plot 9.12.

7. On the question of sex with another person significant differences were found for the comparisons between the male 1.5 generation and the male 2.0 generation (M1.5-M2.0) and the male 1.5 and reference group (M1.5-Mr) with the male 1.5 generation significantly more authoritarian in both comparisons (.05).No comparisons were found to be significant within the female cohort or across gender. See table 9.13 and plot 9.13.

Table 9.1: Tests of Between-Subjects Effects
Dependent Variable: Index Relig3

Source	Type III Sum of Squares	df	Mean Square	F	Sig.	Partial Eta Squared
Corrected Model	29.826ᵃ	7	4.261	28.798	.000	.030
Intercept	9484.294	1	9484.294	64102.075	.000	.907
gender	4.333	1	4.333	29.285	**.000	.004
IGS * gender	.361	3	.120	.813	.486	.000
Error	969.852	6555	.148			
Total	41116.676	6563				
Corrected Total	999.678	6562				

a. R Squared = .030 (Adjusted R Squared = .029)
** = >.001 level

Plot 9.1: Relig3 by gender

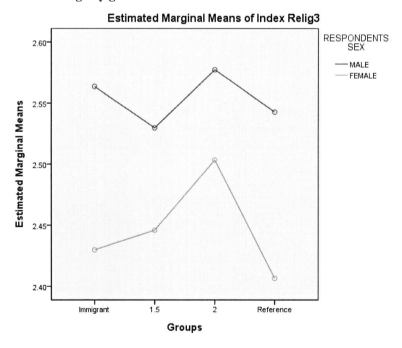

Table 9.2: Tests of Between-Subjects Effects
Dependent Variable: Index BibLit

Source	Type III Sum of Squares	df	Mean Square	F	Sig.	Partial Eta Squared
Corrected Model	20.226ᵃ	7	2.889	12.944	.000	.014
Intercept	12209.986	1	12209.986	54696.238	.000	.893
gender	4.689	1	4.689	21.007	**.000	.003
IGS * gender	.542	3	.181	.810	.488	.000
Error	1459.718	6539	.223			
Total	53066.722	6547				
Corrected Total	1479.945	6546				

a. R Squared = .014 (Adjusted R Squared = .013)
** = >.001 level

Plot 9.2: Biblit3 by gender

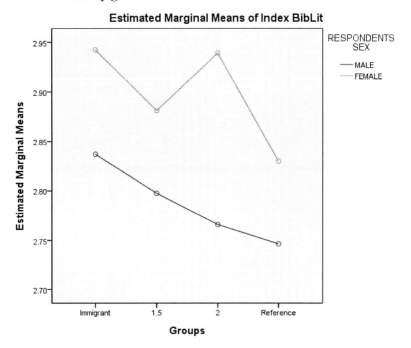

Table 9.3: Tests of Between-Subjects Effects
Dependent Variable: Index Subj3

Source	Type III Sum of Squares	df	Mean Square	F	Sig.	Partial Eta Squared
Corrected Model	93.747[a]	7	13.392	29.355	.000	.030
Intercept	6461.469	1	6461.469	14163.079	.000	.684
gender	11.583	1	11.583	25.388	**.000	.004
IGS * gender	1.600	3	.533	1.169	.320	.001
Error	2987.323	6548	.456			
Total	29191.194	6556				
Corrected Total	3081.071	6555				

a. R Squared = .030 (Adjusted R Squared = .029)
** = >.001 level

Plot 9.3: Subj3 by gender

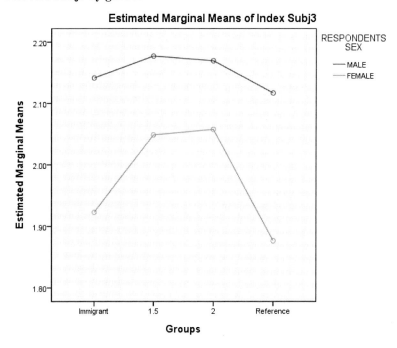

Table 9.4: Tests of Between-Subjects Effects
Dependent Variable: Index Pract3

Source	Type III Sum of Squares	df	Mean Square	F	Sig.	Partial Eta Squared
Corrected Model	99.856ᵃ	7	14.265	21.336	.000	.022
Intercept	10392.299	1	10392.299	15543.054	.000	.704
Gender	21.227	1	21.227	31.747	**.000	.005
IGS * gender	.193	3	.064	.096	.962	.000
Error	4377.414	6547	.669			
Total	49895.694	6555				
Corrected Total	4477.270	6554				

a. R Squared = .022 (Adjusted R Squared = .021)
** = >.001 level

Plot 9.4: Pract3 by gender

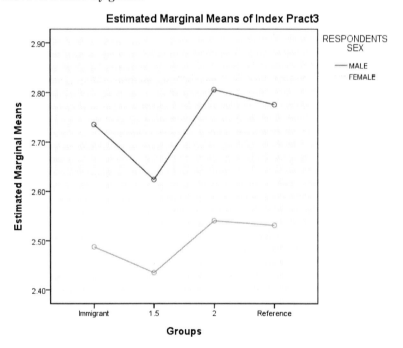

Table 9.5: Tests of Between-Subjects Effects
Dependent Variable: Index Econ3

Source	Type III Sum of Squares	df	Mean Square	F	Sig.	Partial Eta Squared
Corrected Model	112.272[a]	7	16.039	16.338	.000	.026
Intercept	6976.618	1	6976.618	7106.940	.000	.619
gender	6.293	1	6.293	6.411	.741	.001
IGS * gender	1.228	3	.409	.417	.011	.000
Error	4286.921	4367	.982			
Total	37684.806	4375				
Corrected Total	4399.193	4374				

a. R Squared = .026 (Adjusted R Squared = .024)

Plot 9.5: Econ3 by gender

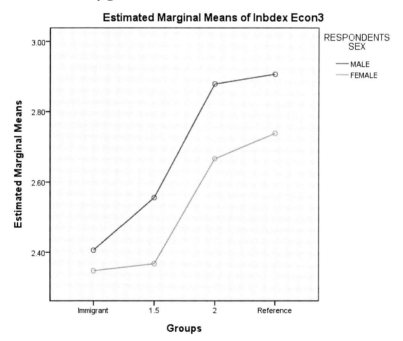

Table 9.6: Tests of Between-Subjects Effects
Dependent Variable: Index Soc7

Source	Type III Sum of Squares	df	Mean Square	F	Sig.	Partial Eta Squared
Corrected Model	20.916[a]	7	2.988	15.428	.000	.016
Intercept	6990.980	1	6990.980	36096.788	.000	.846
gender	3.420	1	3.420	17.659	**.000	.003
IGS * gender	.646	3	.215	1.112	.343	.001
Error	1269.528	6555	.194			
Total	31382.379	6563				
Corrected Total	1290.444	6562				

a. R Squared = .016 (Adjusted R Squared = .015)
** = >.001 level

Plot 9.6: Soc7 by gender

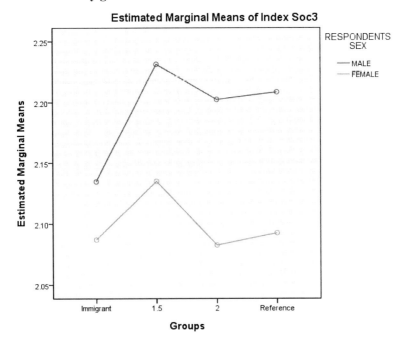

Table 9.7: Tests of Between-Subjects Effects
Dependent Variable: Feelings about pornography laws

Source	Type III Sum of Squares	df	Mean Square	F	Sig.	Partial Eta Squared
Corrected Model	56.784[a]	7	8.112	28.886	.000	.044
Intercept	2984.014	1	2984.014	10625.709	.000	.709
gender	13.256	1	13.256	47.203	.000	.011
IGS * gender	.760	3	.253	.902	.439	.001
Error	1223.294	4356	.281			
Total	13555.000	4364				
Corrected Total	1280.078	4363				

a. R Squared = .044 (Adjusted R Squared = .043)

Plot 9.7: Pornography by gender

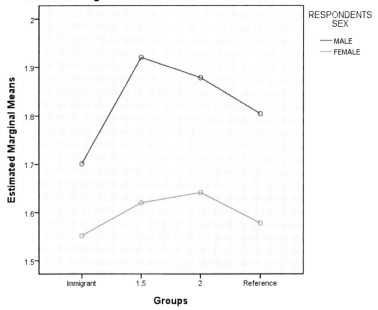

Estimated Marginal Means of FEELINGS ABOUT PORNOGRAPHY LAWS

Table 9.8: Tests of Between-Subjects Effects
Dependent Variable: Homosexual sex relations

Source	Type III Sum of Squares	df	Mean Square	F	Sig.	Partial Eta Squared
Corrected Model	96.269[a]	7	13.753	7.046	.000	.012
Intercept	4859.135	1	4859.135	2489.510	.000	.379
Gender	10.663	1	10.663	5.463	.019	.001
IGS * gender	2.801	3	.934	.478	.697	.000
Error	7951.811	4074	1.952			
Total	29364.000	4082				
Corrected Total	8048.080	4081				

a. R Squared = .012 (Adjusted R Squared = .010)

Plot 9.8: Homosexual sex relations by gender

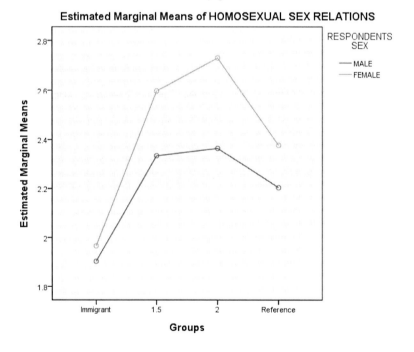

Estimated Marginal Means of HOMOSEXUAL SEX RELATIONS

Table 9.9: Tests of Between-Subjects Effects
Dependent Variable: Homosexuals should have right to marry

Source	Type III Sum of Squares	df	Mean Square	F	Sig.	Partial Eta Squared
Corrected Model	133.041[a]	7	19.006	8.410	.000	.014
Intercept	9663.208	1	9663.208	4275.955	.000	.502
Gender	31.018	1	31.018	13.725	**.000	.003
IGS * gender	15.300	3	5.100	2.257	.080	.002
Error	9581.953	4240	2.260			
Total	54066.000	4248				
Corrected Total	9714.993	4247				

a. R Squared = .014 (Adjusted R Squared = .012)
** = >.001 level

Plot 9.9: Homosexual right to marry by gender

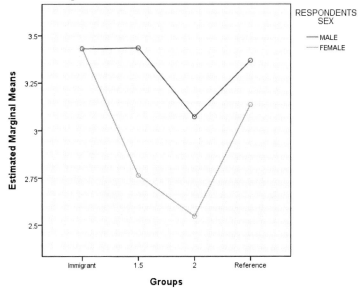

Estimated Marginal Means of HOMOSEXUALS SHOULD HAVE RIGHT TO MARRY

Table 9.10: Tests of Between-Subjects Effects
Dependent Variable: Sex before marriage

Source	Type III Sum of Squares	df	Mean Square	F	Sig.	Partial Eta Squared
Corrected Model	98.870[a]	7	14.124	9.251	.000	.015
Intercept	8536.370	1	8536.370	5591.006	.000	.564
gender	9.470	1	9.470	6.202	.013	.001
IGS * gender	2.444	3	.815	.534	.659	.000
Error	6594.266	4319	1.527			
Total	43693.000	4327				
Corrected Total	6693.137	4326				

a. R Squared = .015 (Adjusted R Squared = .013)

Plot 9.10: Sex before marriage by gender

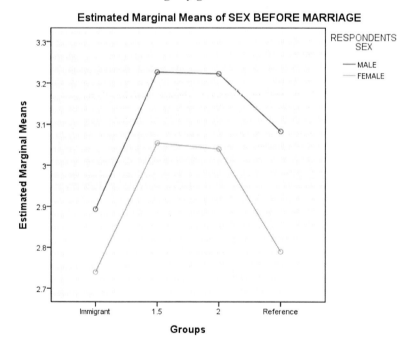

Table 9.11: Tests of Between-Subjects Effects
Dependent Variable: Abortion if woman wants for any reason

Source	Type III Sum of Squares	df	Mean Square	F	Sig.	Partial Eta Squared
Corrected Model	8.505[a]	7	1.215	5.029	.000	.008
Intercept	2383.005	1	2383.005	9862.284	.000	.705
gender	.453	1	.453	1.877	.171	.000
IGS * gender	.878	3	.293	1.211	.304	.001
Error	998.407	4132	.242			
Total	11373.000	4140				
Corrected Total	1006.913	4139				

a. R Squared = .008 (Adjusted R Squared = .007)

Plot 9.11: Abortion by gender

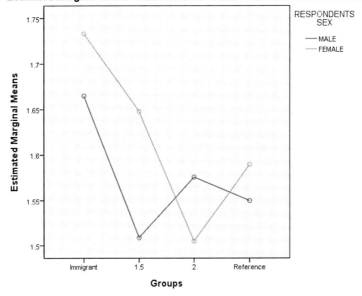

Estimated Marginal Means of ABORTION IF WOMAN WANTS FOR ANY REASON

Table 9.12: Tests of Between-Subjects Effects
Dependent Variable: Divorce laws

Source	Type III Sum of Squares	df	Mean Square	F	Sig.	Partial Eta Squared
Corrected Model	8.022[a]	7	1.146	2.129	.037	.004
Intercept	3352.382	1	3352.382	6228.627	.000	.596
gender	.875	1	.875	1.625	.202	.000
IGS * gender	1.908	3	.636	1.182	.315	.001
Error	2269.143	4216	.538			
Total	18551.000	4224				
Corrected Total	2277.165	4223				

a. R Squared = .004 (Adjusted R Squared = .002)

Plot 9.12: Divorce by gender

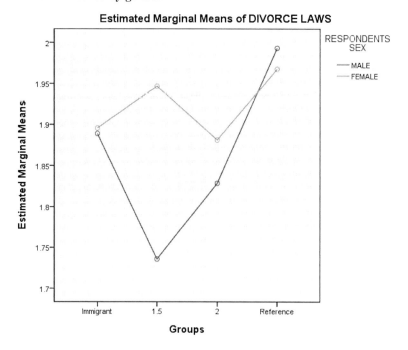

Table 9.13: Tests of Between-Subjects Effects

Dependent Variable: Sex with person other than spouse

Source	Type III Sum of Squares	df	Mean Square	F	Sig.	Partial Eta Squared
Corrected Model	13.571[a]	7	1.939	4.509	.000	.007
Intercept	1753.924	1	1753.924	4079.299	.000	.491
gender	1.202	1	1.202	2.796	.095	.001
IGS * gender	2.631	3	.877	2.040	.106	.001
Error	1817.859	4228	.430			
Total	8913.000	4236				
Corrected Total	1831.430	4235				

a. R Squared = .007 (Adjusted R Squared = .006)

Plot 9.13: Sex with another by gender

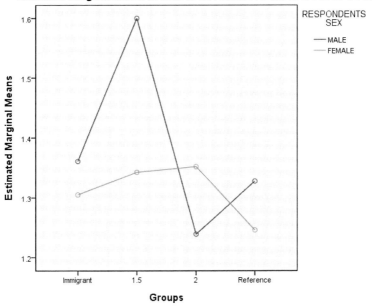

Estimated Marginal Means of SEX WITH PERSON OTHER THAN SPOUSE

CHAPTER TEN

DISCUSSION

This research study tells two interconnected stories. One, a theoretical story that addresses the issue of which paradigm, that of religious orthodoxy (a religious world -view) or a theory of multiple subcultural identities provides the best explanation for predicting and understanding attitudinal patterns expressed in the civil context. This study is supportive of the view that in the real world adherence to salient subcultural identities is fluid and context bound. The second story is that of the post 1965 immigrant and how they utilize sub-cultural identities as tools selected to successfully negotiate their new host environment. This research study was an attempt to understand how theory can be of benefit in understanding the adaptive changes of the post 1965 immigrant flow.

At first glance the intersection of the dependent variable religious orthodoxy (religious intensity) and immigrant generational stage does not tell much about either of our stories. Despite the presence of variability between immigrant generational stages on the aggregate measure of religious orthodox, relig3 (ANOVA =.026), closer analysis (LSD) demonstrated that the majority of the variability was located within the questions addressing issues of biblical literalism. Otherwise very little variability between the immigrant generational stage, 1.5 generation, second-generation, or the reference group on the aggregate measure for religious orthodoxy (relig3) or the core components, of practice or the respondent's subjective sense of religiosity was found. These results were surprising in that I predicted in hypothesis one: *that the immigrant generational stage would be significantly more religiously orthodox than any other group.*

The major portion of the variability indicated by ANOVA and the post hoc analysis was located within questions measuring biblical literalism for comparisons between the immigrant generational stage and the reference group; and again between the second-generation and the reference group. The immigrant generation and the second-generation respondents were more literal in biblical interpretation; more likely than the reference group to respond in the affirmative that god exists, there is an afterlife and that the bible is the definitive word of god. This finding would support my supposition that the immigrant generation is more religiously orthodox, provided we use biblical literalism as the sole measure of religious orthodoxy; with a broader measure of religious orthodoxy we are unable to make this claim. It appears that when taken together as an aggregate measure, the three core indicators are a more sensitive measurement tool of religious orthodoxy or religious intensity, and in all likelihood are measuring different aspects of religious orthodoxy; telling perhaps a different story or component of the story about the relationship between religious orthodoxy and attitudes on economic and social issues.

How do we explain that it is biblical literalism (and not practice or subjective sense of religiosity) that is the primary locus of significant variability between immigrant generational stages? I look to Wuthnow[1] for a partial answer. Wuthnow hypothesized that the western educational process was one that reinforced individualism and modernism. The immigrant generation may simply be more literal in biblical interpretation because of their lack of involvement in the western educational process. Participation in the educational process impacting the immigrants thinking about how to interpret the bible more than affecting praxis or the individual's sense of religiosity.

Yet this does not provide an explanation as to why the second-generation is almost as literal in biblical interpretation as the immigrant generation and significantly more religiously orthodox as measured by the aggregate measure (relig3) than the reference group. One would if Wuthnow was correct, expect the second generation to be significantly less religiously orthodox than the immigrant generation and similar to the reference group on this measure. The educational explanation employed for the immigrant generation does not help. Min (2010)[2] recounts that for the Korean second generation, there is a strong identification with Evangelical Protestantism with a concomitant shift away from a Korean-ethnic church to the Evangelical church. This shift in congregational allegiance has been explained as an attempt at resolving tensions between immigrant generations and as part of the second generation's adaptation to the new country and their developing a separate less ethnic and more religiously intense identity. Thus a shift in congregation or religious affiliation is an acceptable tool utilized in separating sociologically and psychologically from the immigrant generation. This observation of Min's is useful as a possible explanation as to why the second-generation has a scale score on the indices of religious orthodoxy, (as measured by relig3

---

[1] Wurthnow, ibid.
[2] Min, Pyong Gap, ibid.

the aggregate measure of religious orthodoxy) that is on par with the immigrant group yet significantly greater than that of the reference group. See appendix C.1. It seems evident that in the real world multiple explanations must be considered in order to understand the variability in religious orthodoxy (religious intensity) between immigrant generational stages. We begin to see that immigrant generational stages may utilize culture and symbolism as tools to achieve different ends: the second generation making use of the religious intensity of an Evangelical tradition, as a cultural tool, to develop a separate identity from that of the immigrant generation. The immigrant generation utilizing the religiosity of their immigrant church to anchor and support them in their new country.

The story that the data tells at first glance is that there is little in the way of a linear correlation between immigrant generational stages and my broadest measurement of religious orthodox. Specifically, as measured by the aggregate measure of religious orthodoxy, identification with a particular immigrant generational stage is not the most salient reference group orientation in the production of religious orthodoxy. We also begin to develop an awareness for the fact that the selection of subcultural identities as tools to support adaptation is extremely complex due partially to the fluidity of identified ends of our groups and the changing context within which these "cultural tools' are to be used.

Catholic-Protestant Cohort Analysis

When we focus on the intersection of immigrant generation stage and religious tradition on our dependent variable of religious orthodoxy, the relationship between our groups and religious orthodoxy comes in to sharper focus. Analysis was conducted both across religious traditions (Catholics and Protestants) and within religious tradition between immigrant generational stages both for our aggregate measure of religious orthodoxy (relig3) and each of the core components. ANOVA analysis found significant differences across religious traditions for the aggregate measure of religious orthodoxy ($>.001$) but not within religious tradition between immigrant generational stages.

Analysis of the Catholic cohort found great stability between immigrant generational stages. Only for the core component of biblical literalism was a significant difference found and then only for the comparison between the Catholic immigrant generation and the Catholic reference group. The immigrants were again found to be more literal in biblical interpretation. No other comparison was found to be significant for the Catholic cohort between immigrant generational stages on any other measure of religious orthodoxy. The stability of the Catholic cohort makes sense from the perspective that the Catholic Church is a universal church. It possesses a centralized religious hierarchy with the authority to define and interpret doctrine and practice. Its beliefs and practices should be consistent as they are based upon a unified body of church doctrine.

Within the Catholic cohort two trends are noticeable. One appears to be a move towards modernism in regard to biblical literalism between the immigrant generational stage and the catholic reference group. The second is an increase in religious activity or practice between the Catholic immigrant generation and the reference group. It is not possible to say definitively but the decrease in biblical literalism found in the Catholic cohort is most likely a byproduct of exposure to the western educational system. The increase in practice may very well indicate a shift in the type of religious activity, moving away from a family in home practice of an immigrant generation to a community-based institutional practice more in the public sphere. Two of the research questions addressing practice (relactv and relife) may be sensitive to capturing this shift.

Within the Protestant tradition significant differences were found for some comparisons (post hoc analysis) on both the aggregate measure of religious orthodoxy (relig3) and on the measure of religious practice. Specifically, the Protestant immigrant generational stage was found to be more religiously orthodox (relig3) and as having a more active religious life than any other Protestant group. This finding demonstrates support for the hypothesis (at least in the protestant cohort), that immigrants are the most religiously orthodox of all the groups studied.

The measure of Protestant biblical literalism appears stable across immigrant generational stages and significantly less literal than Catholics in all immigrant generational stage comparisons. Protestants are more moderate, less literal in biblical interpretation than Catholics from the beginning and remains so in all comparisons between religious traditions and immigrant generational stages. As noted it would be helpful in our analysis of religious orthodoxy and Protestant immigrant generational stages to know the composition of each immigrant generational stage. How many evangelical or fundamentalists as compared to mainline denominations comprise each of the immigrant generational stages. Unfortunately this data was not available and the modernism noted in our Protestant cohort could be created by a preponderance of mainline Protestant respondents in our sample. One can speculate that this trend towards modernism may be blunted or more pronounced depending on the Protestant cohort composition.

Not only does religion seem to matter but the religious tradition one - self identifies with (subcultural identity or reference group orientation) seems to matter even more. The significance of across religious tradition differences on all measures of religious orthodoxy indicates the variability of religious orthodoxy that exists between religious traditions and underscores the significance of each religious tradition as being a salient reference group orientation for the formation of the religious beliefs, practice and subjective sense of religiosity. It is a better predictor of one's religious orthodoxy or religious intensity to know that a respondent is Catholic or Protestant than what immigrant generation stage he or she is currently in. Our two religious traditions studied appear to be effected differently by immigrant generational stages and each tradition creates adherents whose beliefs and practice are according to my core measures different. The specific immigrant generational stage appears to affect the Catholic cohort less than the Protestant cohort; more variability in the Protestant cohort between immigrant generational stages. This observation is explained as much by the universal nature of the Catholic Church as by the multiplicity of denominations and families with in the Protestant cohort.

Protestants seem to experience a decrease in practice or active religious life when we compare the Protestant immigrant generational stage to the Protestant reference group. This is not so for the Catholic cohort which demonstrates an increase in religious life in the comparisons between Catholic immigrant generational stage and Catholic reference group. How do we understand this bi -directional pattern? For the Catholic cohort could this represent the change in form of religious activity away from an in-home religious practice to a church institutional practice that I have previously suggested? For the Protestant cohort the decrease in religious practice may represent an increase in participation in other organizations that would occur with successful adaptation. Not necessarily representing a decrease in religiosity but more variability in what reference group is considered salient. Again the data does not allow us to answer these questions.

What is clear is that the individual religious traditions have a significant role in how religious beliefs, practice and one's subjective sense of religiosity are expressed. The significant difference found across religious traditions on all measures of religiosity indicates the variability of religious orthodoxy at the intersection of religious tradition and can be interpreted as the significance or salience of religious tradition on their formation.

Gender Cohort Analysis

When we add gender to the analysis and focus upon the intersection of immigrant generational stage and gender on our dependent variable of religious orthodoxy, patterns arise that are similar to those I have identified in our analysis of immigrant generational stage and Catholic and Protestant religious traditions. Analysis was conducted both across gender (male/female) and within gender between immigrant generational stages both for our aggregate measure of religious orthodoxy (relig3) and each core component. ANOVA analysis found significant differences across gender (>.001) but not within gender between immigrant generational stages.

Within gender analysis for the male cohort found great stability between immigrant generational stages and immigrant generational stage appears to have little effect upon male religious orthodoxy. In fact ANOVA indicated a lack of significant difference between male immigrant generational stages on all of our measures of religious orthodoxy. When we compare the male immigrant generation to the male reference group we do note a gradual shift towards modernism within the male cohort on our measure of the biblical literalism. Within the male cohort the locus of variability is within questions assessing religious practice where the male second-generation and male reference group demonstrated an increase in religious life. Globally, religious life and participation is increasingly important for men in our study.

Within gender analysis for the female cohort found greater variability particularly for the female second-generation. Here we observed spikes or increases in relig3, biblit3 and subj3; but not interestingly, in practice. Females demonstrated less religious practice than males in all immigrant generation stages. Does this tell us that although females continue to be religious as a cohort, church activity and power within church institutions are gender contested? I believe that this is an accurate interpretation and that the data indicates the significance of church activity for males at the possible exclusion of female religious.

Across gender analysis found that in general males were more religiously orthodox than the female cohort on all comparisons. Males are more active in their religious life and they perceive it that way. It is in the area of biblical literalism across gender, that we find a significant difference within the female immigrant and female second-generation groups. Here both female groups are significantly more literal in biblical interpretation than their male comparisons. This may indicate the role of woman in society and the task of socializing the next generation through a more traditional stance on family values and greater reliance on biblical literalism as a guidepost.

Given that significant differences across gender were noted on all measures of religious orthodoxy the variability of religious orthodoxy at the intersection of gender is supported; emphasizing the significance of gender as a salient reference group orientation for the formation of beliefs, practice, and subjective sense of religiosity.

Economic Issues

The literature on the relationship between economic issues and religious orthodoxy is mixed and suggests two opposing positions. One that a religious worldview (moral cosmology) or in our case, religious orthodoxy, is not correlated to attitudes on economic issues. Here religious orthodoxy or worldview is perceived as being one of many reference group orientations or sub-cultural identities and not sufficiently salient to be the primary life lenses that provides justification for economic opinions. The alternative position is that there is a strong correlation between religious orthodoxy and stances on economic issues: specifically that religious orthodoxy is associated with a sense of community and civic responsibility towards others leading to a communitarian economic stance. In our analysis of religious orthodoxy and immigrant generational stages we found that the Catholic and Protestant religious traditions and gender were salient in the creation of patterns of beliefs, practice and one's subjective sense of religiosity; the immigrant generational stage of the respondent less so. In the creation of stances for issues of economic concern, immigrant generational stage has primacy.

The Pearson Rho test of significant correlations was used on the data set to determine the presence or absence of significant correlations or relationships between religious orthodoxy and economic stances within our study sample. Rho correlations indicated the absence of significant correlation between these two dependent variables. No significant correlation was detected for relig3 the aggregate measure of religiosity or its core components for any of our groups (immigrant generational stages) or at the intersection of immigrant generational stage and religious tradition (Catholic/Protestant) or gender. Thus it seems clear; we must look elsewhere for salient reference group orientations that are associated with economic opinions. Religious beliefs, practice and one's subjective sense of religiosity is not sufficiently salient to create attitudes or stances on economic issues.

Our second Hypothesis predicted *that the immigrant generational stage will be more communitarian on economic issues by virtue of their strong religious beliefs.* ANOVA analysis found significant relationships or correlations between our groups or immigrant generational stages such that the immigrant generation and the 1.5 generation were more communitarian on economic issues then the second generation or reference group. This finding was present in both religious traditions (Catholic/Protestant) as is visible in plot 8.5. Moreover when economic opinions were analyzed at the intersection of immigrant generational stage and religious tradition (Catholic/Protestant), no significant differences were found across the religious traditions. Irrespective of religious traditions, the immigrant generational stage and the 1.5 generation convey a stance of responsibility to and from others that is significantly greater than the second generation's or reference groups.

A similar division between the immigrant generational stage and the 1.5 generation and the second generation and reference group was found at the intersection of immigrant generational stage and gender on economic issues. Significant differences within immigrant generational stages were found, again indicating that within both genders the immigrant and 1.5 generation are statistically more communitarian. No significant difference was noticeable across gender. I take this finding as indicating that the salient drivers or reference group orientation, for economic opinions, are different from those that are salient for the creation of religious orthodoxy. For economic opinions what appears to be the salient reference group orientation is immigrant generational stage. For religious orthodoxy, the religious tradition one- self identifies with and one's gender act as reference group orientations or subcultural identities that play a defining role in the creation of respondents religious orthodoxy. Our data follows a logical course. Immigrants and 1.5 generation are clearly faced with the task of successfully negotiating the barriers which exist in their adaptation to the new host environment. It makes sense that they would look towards others as well as institutions for resources and support in this process. This is the case whether one is male or female; Catholic or Protestant.

What is now needed is the opportunity to have conversations with immigrant respondents to verify and develop a more in-depth understanding of the above suppositions. This unfortunately exceeds the scope of this study and must await next steps. What appears clear from the data is that for stances on economic issues religious beliefs, self-identified religious tradition or gender are not the most salient subcultural identity to create tools for successful adaptation. Immigrant generation and the 1.5 generation are more communitarian on economic issues based upon the practical demands of their everyday life. By virtue of their being immigrants and new to the host environment they need and look to others for support and resources. Subcultural identities or reference group orientations are the tools that aid in the development of attitudes and opinions expressed in their life world, that the immigrant believes will be helpful or necessary for their successful adaptation into the host society. The salience of subcultural identities or reference group orientations shift over the course of their adaptation creating patterns in civil society that are supportive of the tasks immigrants must address.

Social Issues

According to Wuthnow[3], Hunter[4] and Davis and Stark[5] a religious world view such as the theory of moral cosmology correlates authoritarian stances on social issues to religious orthodoxy. Simply, the greater the degree of religious orthodoxy (religious intensity) the more authoritarian one's stance becomes on social concerns. The indices soc7 is the aggregate measurement for social issues, capturing where a respondent falls on a continuum of authoritarianism-modernism for substantive issues of social concern. It is interpreted as the degree to which a respondent views decisions made about social issues residing within the percepts of religious beliefs rather than within the individual. We have seen that religious tradition and gender are salient for the production of religious orthodoxy. For stances on economic issues the immigrant generational stage has constitutive power. However in the deconstruction of the relationship between immigrant generational stages , religious tradition and gender and stances on issues of social concern a more complex analysis presents itself that does not yield readily to identifiable patterns for interpretation.

The Pearson Rho test of significant correlations was used on the data set to determine the presence or absence of significant correlations or relationships between religious orthodoxy and stances on social issues. No significant correlation was detected for relig3, the aggregate measure of religiosity or its core components, with any of our groups (immigrant generational stages) or the intersection of immigrant generation stage and religious tradition or gender for the aggregate measure (soc7). This is an unexpected and puzzling finding as I had predicted in hypothesis number three that: *a religious worldview or religious orthodoxy as expressed by the theory of Moral Cosmology is viable and the most salient*

---

[3] Wurthnow, ibid.
[4] Hunter, ibid.
[5] Davis and Stark, ibid.

explanatory theory in predicting the stances on economic and social issues for the post-1965 immigrant population. I have some hesitancy in taking a strong position on this finding as the percentage of fundamentalists or evangelicals in the Protestant cohort or the conservative Catholics in the catholic cohort are unknown in our sample. I am on more solid footing stating that I cannot demonstrate religious Orthodox to be sufficiently salient to produce stances on issues of social concern. Again we need to look for other subcultural identities or reference group orientations that act as justification or motivation for the creation of expressed opinions on social issues.

On first look, ANOVA analysis found little variability between groups or immigrant generational stages and our aggregate measure of social concerns (soc7). This could be attributable to a preponderance of Main line and moderate Catholics shaping our data. I cannot state this definitively as the data was not aggregated in this fashion in order to obtain healthy cell size in each immigrant generational stage. Considerable variability was noted for all seven questions comprising this measure as well as for specific comparisons within some of the questions (LSD). Unfortunately there appears to be no clear or discernible pattern in the relationship between immigrant generational stage and stance on social issues. Some immigrant generational stages are more authoritarian on certain questions and less so on others; for example the immigrant generational stage was more authoritarian on the questions addressing abortion and the homosexuals right to marry; less authoritarian on questions addressing pornography and sex before marriage. Generally speaking, the relationship between immigrant generational stages and stances on issues of social concern is weak and does not count for the variability observed.

When we focus on the intersection of immigrant generational stage and religious tradition (Catholic/Protestant) on our dependent variable for social concerns, the relationship between our groups (immigrant generational stages) and social concerns becomes more complex. Analysis was conducted both across religious traditions (Catholic and Protestant) and within religious tradition between immigrant generational stages both for our aggregate measure of social concern (soc7) and for each of the seven questions comprising the indices. ANOVA analysis found significant variability both across religious tradition and within religious tradition between immigrant generational stages. Religious tradition matters and may matter more than a respondents degree of religious orthodoxy or religious intensity in the formation of attitudes and opinions on issues of social concern. Significant differences were found across religious traditions on the aggregate measure of social concerns (soc7) and for 6 out of the seven questions that comprise the indices. No significant difference was found between religious traditions on the question addressing a woman's rights to seek an abortion.

For certain questions the Protestant cohort was more authoritarian for others the Catholic cohort were more authoritarian. Again I am on safer grounds stating that adherents to a specific religious tradition (in our study Catholicism or Protestantism) have significantly different opinions on issues of social concerns that are attributable to the religious tradition that they self identify with, then attempting to interpret and identify causality for their responses.

Furthermore there appears to be an interactive effect between immigrant generational stage and religious tradition on issues of social concern that creates additional significant variability in our responses. The analysis of within religious tradition between immigrant generational stages for stances on social concerns does not yield readily to identifiable patterns that may be viewed as motivation or justification for individual action. Four of the questions comprising the indices of social concern (abortion, divorce, homosexual sex relationship and sex before marriage) yielded significance differences within religious tradition between immigrant generational stages, and the responses were not uni-directional.

Globally speaking there is less variability within the Protestant cohort between the immigrant generational stages and a trend towards modernism. This trend towards Protestant modernism is most evident on the aggregate measure (soc7). The Catholic cohort appears to be influenced more by immigrant generational stages as is evidenced by the existence of greater variability of the responses to social issues of concern between the immigrant generational stages. Again globally speaking Catholics seem to demonstrate a trend towards greater authoritarianism and away from modernism, as is evidenced by the Catholic reference group being significantly more authoritarian on our aggregate measure of social concern then the Catholic immigrant generation.

Variability persists when we focus on the intersection of immigrant generational stage and gender on our dependent variable measuring social concerns. Analysis was conducted both across gender (male and female) and within gender between immigrant generational stages for both our aggregate measure of social concern (Soc7) and for each of the seven questions comprising the indices. ANOVA analysis (soc7) indicated significant difference across gender (.>001) but the absence of significant within gender differences between immigrant generational stages. Both the female and male cohort demonstrated little variability between immigrant generational stages on the aggregate measure or any of the seven questions comprising the aggregate measure. This is especially noticeable in the female cohort where immigrant generational stages seem to matter very little.

In general the male cohort was more authoritarian on issues of social concern than the female cohort for all immigrant generational stages; but not significantly so. There appears to be a trend towards authoritarianism in the male cohort with the male reference group more authoritarian than the immigrant generational stage. It must be with hesitation that I make this observation as I am limited by not knowing the religious tradition composition of the male cohort or for the immigrant generational stages. The male cohort could be more authoritarian by virtue of an interactive effect between the male gender and Catholic religious tradition (the Catholic reference group being significantly more authoritarian than the Catholic immigrant generational stage). We were unable to test for the significance of this interaction. However I am comfortable in interpreting the data as indicative of multiple subcultural identities or reference group orientations, motivating and justifying the expression of attitudes or opinions for social issues.

In the analysis across gender significant difference was found for four of our seven questions; pornography, homosexual sex relationship, homosexual's right to marriage, and sex before marriage. The male cohort was more authoritarian for pornography, homosexual's right to marriage, sex before marriage; the female cohort was more authoritarian on the issue of homosexuality (homosexual sex relations). The significant variability between gender and lack of a clear response pattern on these questions is indicative of the complex nature of the relationship and the difficulty of understanding and interpreting what may be acting as motivation and justification for these opinions.

For example, the issue of the male cohort being significantly more authoritarian (having a stronger prohibition) than the female cohort against pornography in all immigrant generational stages seems counterintuitive. One would expect that the female cohort would express a stronger prohibition against pornography due to a feminist perspective that pornography is abusive to women. Likewise, I found it puzzling that males have a stricter prohibition against premarital sex than the female cohort and females express a stronger prohibition against homosexuality itself but are more modernist in their opinion that homosexuals should have the right to marriage. Unfortunately the answers to these puzzling questions are not yet available. They are to be found in future conversations with the post 1965 immigrant population that unfortunately lye beyond the scope of this study.

CHAPTER ELEVEN

CONCLUSIONS

Hypothesis One:
The immigrant generational stage will be more religiously orthodox than the reference group and all other target groups

Hypothesis one was not supported. Based upon comparisons made between immigrant generational stages and utilizing the aggregate measure of religious orthodoxy the immigrant generational stage was not found to be statistically more religiously orthodox than all other target groups or the reference group. In fact the aggregate measure of religious orthodoxy indicates little variability between immigrant generational stages on this dependent variable. However the immigrant generational stage was most literal in biblical interpretation. This was found to be so for immigrant generational stages in both the male and female cohorts but not within the Catholic and Protestant religious traditions.

Hypothesis Two:
The immigrant generation stage will be more communitarian on economic issues and more authoritarian on social issues (looking towards religious doctrine to define economic and acceptable social behavior) than any other target group or the reference group

Hypothesis Two was not supported. Hypothesis Two has two components: A) that by virtue of their religious orthodoxy or religious intensity the immigrant generational stage will be most communitarian on economic issues and B) most authoritarian on stances on social issues. Concerning stances on economic issues, the immigrant generational stage and the 1.5 generation were found to be more communitarian but based upon their life demands as being immigrants and new to the host society. Religious orthodoxy was not found to be correlated to economic issues. For the dependent variable addressing stances on social concerns, the immigrant generational stage was not consistent in developing the most authoritarian stance. Religious orthodoxy was again found not to be correlated to social issues.

Hypothesis Three:
A religious worldview or religious orthodoxy as expressed by the theory of Moral Cosmology is viable as the most salient explanatory theory in predicting the stances on economic and social issues of the post-1965 immigrant population

Hypothesis three was not supported. Religious orthodoxy or religious worldview is one of many subcultural identities; beliefs, practice, and the subjective sense of religiosity do not grow in a vacuum but are the productions of other subcultural identities or reference group orientations i.e., education, gender, or specific religious tradition. Religious orthodoxy is not a standalone construct. The behavior and cognitive patterns that expresses an individual's religious orthodoxy or religious intensity are the cultural tools put to use by the individual for the successful attainment of life goals. These patterns are variable in salience, fluid, context bound and dependent upon real-life issues.

Hypothesis Four:
Significant variability will be found across religious traditions (Protestant and Catholic) for the dependent variables, religious orthodoxy, social and economic issues. However, variability on social and economic issues will be correlated to the degree of religious orthodoxy or religious intensity and not correlated to a religious tradition (Catholic/Protestant)

Hypothesis four was not supported. Significant differences were found across religious tradition (Catholic/Protestant) for both of the dependent variables, religious orthodoxy and stances on social issues. However research data was unable to establish a significant correlation between religious orthodoxy and stances on social issues; meaning that measuring an individual's beliefs, practice, and subjective sense of religiosity is not (in itself) helpful in predicting stances on social issues. Nevertheless Catholics and Protestants are different in the positions they take on substantive issues of social concern. I interpret this as the significance of salient subcultural identity/reference group orientations (other than religious worldview or religious orthodoxy) in shaping these stances and as being supportive of the role of multiple intersecting subcultural identities. No significant difference was found across religious tradition (Catholic/protestant) for stances on economic issues. In fact both religious traditions demonstrated a similar profile on economic issues with the immigrant generational stage and the 1.5 generation being most communitarian. Again I find support for salient subcultural identities (here immigrant status) other than religious worldview.

Hypothesis Five:
Significant variability will be found across gender for the dependent variables religious orthodoxy, social and economic issues. However variability on social and economic issues will be correlated to degree of religious orthodoxy or religious intensity and not correlated to gender

Hypothesis five was not supported. Significant differences were found across gender for both of the dependent variables religious orthodoxy and social issues, with research data once again being unable to establish a significant correlation between religious orthodoxy (religious intensity) and stances on social issues. Similar to the Catholic and Protestant religious traditions, gender demonstrated differences on their positions taken on stances for social issues. I interpret this again as the significance of gender as a salient subcultural identity/reference group orientation in the creation of stances on substantial issues of social concern. Again as with religious tradition no significant difference was found across gender for stances on economic issues: the immigrant generational stage and the 1.5 generation being communitarian in both genders.

Epilogue

Although religious beliefs, practices and one's subjective sense of religiosity are common to all expressions of religion, I have found that religious orthodoxy is not a unified and monolithic construct. Religious orthodoxy or religious intensity in this study is nuanced by the most salient sub- cultural identities or reference group orientations holding sway at any given moment in time. In this study I have made the case that it is the intersection of beliefs, practice and one's subjective sense of religiosity with the subcultural identities of immigrant generational stage, religious tradition (Catholic/Protestant) and gender that produces in the public sphere opinions or stances on issues of economic and social concerns. However salient subcultural identities could just as readily be race, social class or feminism.

As Alba, Raboteau and DeWind have captured in a story of a multi-generational Korean- American Buddhist family, the Buddhist position of free choice is called upon to make free choice decisions about what religious tradition a second generation son can identify with but was not a salient tradition employed as a cultural tool when it came time for the son's marital decisions (2009: 180)[1]. Life course developmental issues produce stress and require cultural tools for adaptation that must be fluid and provide options that the individual believes will be of value and lead to success. Religious orthodoxy when viewed at the intersection of other subcultural identities is expressed in diverse and changing ways that challenges simple assumptions about its relationship to real world issues.

This study focused upon the intersection of religious orthodoxy and subcultural identity in creating civil life. Although I have attempted not to lose sight of individual agency within the locus of a larger systemic frame, I am not totally convinced that I have succeeded. Admittedly this study is a first look at patterns and cognitions at play in the public sphere. It calls for the real life stories that inhabit life in civil society to be told.

---

[1] Alba, Richard, Raboteau, Albert and DeWind,Josh, (2009). *Immigration and religion in America*, New York University.

APPENDIX A

QUESTIONS COMPRISING THE INDICES OF RELIGIOUS ORTHODOXY

Biblical literalism

(Bible) Bible word of god
(God) God exists
(Post-life) belief in afterlife

Practice

(Pray) How often do you pray
(Relactiv) How often do you take part in religious activities
(Relife) Try to carry beliefs into activities

Subjective

(Relpersn) Consider self a religious person
(Reliten) Strength of religious affiliation
(Relexper) religious experience changed life

All nine questions are found in the 2006, 2008 and 2010 GSS waves.

APPENDIX B

QUESTIONS COMPRISING THE INDICES FOR ECONOMIC AND SOCIAL ISSUES

All questions asked on the GSS 2006, 2008, 2010.

Questions: Economic

1. helppoor – should the government improve the standard of living
2. helpnot – should the government do more or less to solve our countries problems
3. helpsick – should the government help pay for medical care

Questions: Social

1. Abany – abortion if a woman wants for any reason
2. Divlaw – should divorce in this country be easier or more difficult to obtain than it is now
3. Xmarsex – what is your opinion about a married person having sexual relations with someone other than their marriage partner
4. Premarsex – sex before marriage
5. Pornlaw – feelings about pornography laws
6. Homosex – homosexual sex relations
7. Marhomo – homosexuals should have right to marry

All ten questions are found in the 2006, 2008, 2010 GSS waves.

APPENDIX C.1

INDICES SCORES FOR RELIGIOUS ORTHODOXY BY MAIN GROUPS (IGS)

Groups		Biblit3	Pract3	Subj3	religos3	econ3	soc7	ABORTION IF WOMAN WANTS FOR ANY REASON	DIVORCE LAWS	SEX WITH PERSON OTHER THAN SPOUSE	FEELINGS ABOUT PORNOGRAPHY LAWS	HOMOSEXUAL SEX RELATIONS	HOMOSEXUALS SHOULD HAVE RIGHT TO MARRY	SEX BEFORE MARRIAGE
1	Mean	2.89	2.60	2.02	2.49	2.37	2.11	1.70	1.89	1.33	1.62	1.93	3.43	2.81
	N	601	603	601	603	400	604	370	372	383	395	350	380	397
2	Mean	2.84	2.52	2.11	2.48	2.45	2.18	1.59	1.86	1.46	1.75	2.48	3.07	3.13
	N	208	209	209	209	144	208	128	128	133	142	124	134	126
3	Mean	2.87	2.65	2.10	2.53	2.75	2.13	1.53	1.86	1.31	1.74	2.58	2.75	3.12
	N	268	270	270	270	178	271	169	171	175	180	166	176	172
4	Mean	2.79	2.64	1.98	2.47	2.81	2.14	1.57	1.98	1.28	1.68	2.30	3.24	2.92
	N	5470	5473	5476	5481	3653	5480	3473	3553	3545	3647	3442	3558	3632
Total	Mean	2.81	2.63	2.00	2.47	2.76	2.14	1.58	1.96	1.29	1.68	2.29	3.23	2.92
	N	6547	6555	6556	6563	4375	6563	4140	4224	4236	4364	4082	4248	4327

APPENDIX C.2

INDICES SCORES FOR RELIGIOUS ORTHODOXY BY MAIN GROUPS (IGS) AND RELIGIOUS TRADITION

Groups	Catholic or Protestant		Biblit3	Pract3	Subj3	religos3	econ3	soc7	ABORTION IF WOMAN WANTS FOR ANY REASON	DIVORCE LAWS	SEX WITH PERSON OTHER THAN SPOUSE	FEELINGS ABOUT PORNOGRAPHY LAWS	HOMOSEXUAL SEX RELATIONS	HOMOSEXUALS SHOULD HAVE RIGHT TO MARRY	SEX BEFORE MARRIAGE
1	Catholic	Mean	3.00	2.40	1.92	2.42	2.34	2.08	1.81	1.73	1.26	1.58	1.77	3.36	2.91
		N	291	291	291	291	196	291	177	183	184	194	162	178	194
	Protestant	Mean	2.80	2.78	1.70	2.42	2.40	2.10	1.69	2.05	1.33	1.58	1.75	3.85	2.53
		N	152	152	151	152	105	152	91	96	93	103	89	94	99
	Total	Mean	2.93	2.53	1.84	2.42	2.37	2.08	1.77	1.84	1.29	1.58	1.76	3.53	2.78
		N	443	443	442	443	301	443	268	279	277	297	251	272	293
2	Catholic	Mean	2.93	2.38	1.90	2.39	2.49	2.15	1.56	1.70	1.46	1.78	2.33	3.16	3.21
		N	103	103	103	103	77	102	66	63	68	76	64	69	56
	Protestant	Mean	2.75	2.41	1.65	2.27	2.39	2.17	1.72	2.15	1.19	1.73	2.00	3.56	2.81
		N	45	45	45	45	29	45	25	33	26	30	23	25	31
	Total	Mean	2.88	2.39	1.82	2.35	2.47	2.16	1.60	1.87	1.38	1.76	2.24	3.27	3.07
		N	148	148	148	148	106	147	91	96	94	106	87	94	87
3	Catholic	Mean	2.94	2.55	1.93	2.46	2.85	2.06	1.58	1.80	1.25	1.75	2.34	2.89	2.86
		N	137	137	137	137	92	137	89	85	92	92	86	92	83
	Protestant	Mean	2.84	2.62	1.80	2.41	2.73	2.08	1.52	1.87	1.16	1.52	2.27	3.16	2.97
		N	49	49	49	49	31	49	29	31	33	33	30	31	32
	Total	Mean	2.91	2.57	1.90	2.45	2.82	2.07	1.57	1.82	1.23	1.69	2.32	2.96	2.89
		N	186	186	186	186	123	186	118	116	123	125	116	123	115
4	Catholic	Mean	2.87	2.54	1.91	2.43	2.94	2.21	1.59	1.97	1.28	1.72	2.61	3.00	3.21
		N	998	998	998	998	676	998	611	652	626	678	594	625	671
	Protestant	Mean	2.82	2.58	1.69	2.36	2.84	2.07	1.65	2.00	1.20	1.57	1.91	3.62	2.59
		N	3135	3137	3139	3140	2089	3137	2013	2030	2064	2079	2013	2069	2048
	Total	Mean	2.83	2.57	1.74	2.37	2.86	2.10	1.64	1.99	1.22	1.61	2.07	3.48	2.75
		N	4133	4135	4137	4138	2765	4135	2624	2682	2690	2757	2607	2694	2719
Total	Catholic	Mean	2.90	2.50	1.91	2.43	2.79	2.17	1.63	1.90	1.29	1.70	2.41	3.07	3.13
		N	1529	1529	1529	1529	1041	1528	943	973	970	1040	906	964	1004
	Protestant	Mean	2.82	2.59	1.69	2.36	2.81	2.07	1.65	2.00	1.20	1.58	1.91	3.62	2.60
		N	3381	3383	3384	3386	2254	3383	2158	2190	2214	2245	2155	2219	2210
	Total	Mean	2.85	2.56	1.76	2.38	2.80	2.10	1.64	1.97	1.23	1.62	2.06	3.45	2.76
		N	4910	4912	4913	4915	3295	4911	3101	3163	3184	3285	3061	3183	3214

APPENDIX C.3

INDICES SCORES FOR RELIGIOUS ORTHODOXY BY MAIN GROUPS (IGS) AND GENDER

Groups	RESPONDENTS SEX		Biblit3	Pract3	Subj3	religos3	econ3	soc7	ABORTION IF WOMAN WANTS FOR ANY REASON	DIVORCE LAWS	SEX WITH PERSON OTHER THAN SPOUSE	FEELINGS ABOUT PORNOGRAPHY LAWS	HOMOSEXUAL SEX RELATIONS	HOMOSEXUALS SHOULD HAVE RIGHT TO MARRY	SEX BEFORE MARRIAGE
1	MALE	Mean	2.84	2.74	2.14	2.56	2.41	2.13	1.66	1.89	1.36	1.70	1.90	3.43	2.89
		N	277	278	277	278	179	278	179	171	183	174	175	186	178
	FEMALE	Mean	2.94	2.49	1.92	2.43	2.35	2.09	1.73	1.90	1.31	1.55	1.97	3.43	2.74
		N	324	325	324	325	221	325	191	201	200	221	175	194	219
	Total	Mean	2.89	2.60	2.02	2.49	2.37	2.11	1.70	1.89	1.33	1.62	1.93	3.43	2.81
		N	601	603	601	603	400	603	370	372	383	395	350	380	397
2	MALE	Mean	2.80	2.62	2.18	2.53	2.56	2.23	1.51	1.74	1.60	1.92	2.33	3.44	3.23
		N	93	93	93	93	66	92	57	53	60	63	57	62	53
	FEMALE	Mean	2.88	2.44	2.05	2.45	2.37	2.14	1.65	1.95	1.34	1.62	2.60	2.76	3.05
		N	115	116	116	116	78	116	71	75	73	79	67	72	73
	Total	Mean	2.84	2.52	2.11	2.48	2.45	2.18	1.59	1.86	1.46	1.75	2.48	3.07	3.13
		N	208	209	209	209	144	208	128	128	133	142	124	134	126
3	MALE	Mean	2.77	2.81	2.17	2.58	2.88	2.20	1.58	1.83	1.24	1.88	2.36	3.07	3.22
		N	109	109	109	109	73	110	66	70	67	74	66	68	72
	FEMALE	Mean	2.94	2.54	2.06	2.50	2.67	2.08	1.50	1.88	1.35	1.64	2.73	2.55	3.04
		N	159	161	161	161	105	161	103	101	108	106	100	108	100
	Total	Mean	2.87	2.65	2.10	2.53	2.75	2.13	1.53	1.86	1.31	1.74	2.58	2.75	3.12
		N	268	270	270	270	178	271	169	171	175	180	166	176	172
4	MALE	Mean	2.75	2.78	2.12	2.54	2.91	2.21	1.55	1.99	1.33	1.80	2.20	3.37	3.08
		N	2415	2419	2423	2424	1609	2426	1526	1585	1563	1605	1531	1575	1621
	FEMALE	Mean	2.83	2.53	1.88	2.41	2.74	2.09	1.59	1.97	1.25	1.58	2.38	3.14	2.79
		N	3055	3054	3053	3057	2044	3054	1947	1968	1982	2042	1911	1983	2011
	Total	Mean	2.79	2.64	1.98	2.47	2.81	2.14	1.57	1.98	1.28	1.68	2.30	3.24	2.92
		N	5470	5473	5476	5481	3653	5480	3473	3553	3545	3647	3442	3558	3632
Total	MALE	Mean	2.76	2.77	2.12	2.55	2.85	2.20	1.56	1.97	1.34	1.80	2.18	3.37	3.07
		N	2894	2899	2904	2904	1927	2907	1828	1879	1873	1916	1829	1891	1924
	FEMALE	Mean	2.85	2.52	1.89	2.41	2.69	2.09	1.60	1.96	1.26	1.58	2.37	3.12	2.80
		N	3653	3656	3654	3659	2448	3656	2312	2345	2363	2448	2253	2357	2403
	Total	Mean	2.81	2.63	2.00	2.47	2.76	2.14	1.58	1.96	1.29	1.68	2.29	3.23	2.92
		N	6547	6555	6556	6563	4375	6563	4140	4224	4236	4364	4082	4248	4327

APPENDIX D.1

PEARSON RHO CORRELATIONS BETWEEN MAIN GROUPS (IGS) AND DEPENDENT VARIABLES

Immigrants

Descriptive Statistics

	Mean	Std. Deviation	N
Index BibLit	2.8938	.59445	601
Index Pract3	2.6020	.82876	603
Index Subj3	2.0236	.62037	601
Index Relig3	2.4916	.38494	603
Inbdex Econ3	2.3738	.93775	400
Index Soc3	2.1091	.46587	604

Correlations

		Index BibLit	Index Pract3	Index Subj3	Index Relig3	Index Econ3	Index Soc7
Index BibLit	Pearson Correlation	1	-.170**	-.062	.236**	-.021	-.032
	Sig. (2-tailed)		.000	.129	.000	.675	.436
	N	601	601	599	601	400	601
Index Pract3	Pearson Correlation	-.170**	1	.183**	.750**	.082	.048
	Sig. (2-tailed)	.000		.000	.000	.101	.241
	N	601	603	601	603	400	603
Index Subj3	Pearson Correlation	-.062	.183**	1	.640**	.060	.166**
	Sig. (2-tailed)	.129	.000		.000	.234	.000
	N	599	601	601	601	399	601
Index Relig3	Pearson Correlation	.236**	.750**	.640**	1	.083	.118**
	Sig. (2-tailed)	.000	.000	.000		.099	.004
	N	601	603	601	603	400	603
Index Econ3	Pearson Correlation	-.021	.082	.060	.083	1	.004
	Sig. (2-tailed)	.675	.101	.234	.099		.936
	N	400	400	399	400	400	400
Index Soc7	Pearson Correlation	-.032	.048	.166**	.118**	.004	1
	Sig. (2-tailed)	.436	.241	.000	.004	.936	
	N	601	603	601	603	400	604

**. Correlation is significant at the 0.01 level (2-tailed).

1.5 Generation

Descriptive Statistics

	Mean	Std. Deviation	N
Index BibLit	2.8438	.54534	208
Index Pract3	2.5191	.81085	209
Index Subj3	2.1061	.69264	209
Index Relig3	2.4833	.40165	209
Inbdex Econ3	2.4537	.80269	144
Index Soc3	2.1777	.44577	208

Correlations

		Index BibLit	Index Pract3	Index Subj3	Index Relig3	Index Econ3	Index Soc7
Index BibLit	Pearson Correlation	1	-.097	-.153*	.169*	.034	.006
	Sig. (2-tailed)		.162	.027	.015	.686	.928
	N	208	208	208	208	144	207
Index Pract3	Pearson Correlation	-.097	1	.259**	.774**	-.013	.003
	Sig. (2-tailed)	.162		.000	.000	.876	.969
	N	208	209	209	209	144	208
Index Subj3	Pearson Correlation	-.153*	.259**	1	.708**	.039	.126
	Sig. (2-tailed)	.027	.000		.000	.645	.069
	N	208	209	209	209	144	208
Index Relig3	Pearson Correlation	.169*	.774**	.708**	1	.028	.079
	Sig. (2-tailed)	.015	.000	.000		.738	.256
	N	208	209	209	209	144	208
Index Econ3	Pearson Correlation	.034	-.013	.039	.028	1	.088
	Sig. (2-tailed)	.686	.876	.645	.738		.293
	N	144	144	144	144	144	144
Index Soc7	Pearson Correlation	.006	.003	.126	.079	.088	1
	Sig. (2-tailed)	.928	.969	.069	.256	.293	
	N	207	208	208	208	144	208

*. Correlation is significant at the 0.05 level (2-tailed).
**. Correlation is significant at the 0.01 level (2-tailed).

Appendix D.1

2nd Generation

Descriptive Statistics

	Mean	Std. Deviation	N
Index BibLit	2.8688	.52476	268
Index Pract3	2.6475	.91453	270
Index Subj3	2.1031	.58954	270
Index Relig3	2.5332	.38987	270
Inbdex Econ3	2.7537	1.05472	178
Index Soc3	2.1313	.41818	271

Correlations

		Index BibLit	Index Pract3	Index Subj3	Index Relig3	Index Econ3	Index Soc7
Index BibLit	Pearson Correlation	1	-.184**	.000	.217**	.035	.013
	Sig. (2-tailed)		.003	.996	.000	.648	.834
	N	268	268	268	268	176	268
Index Pract3	Pearson Correlation	-.184**	1	.115	.771**	-.054	.103
	Sig. (2-tailed)	.003		.060	.000	.479	.092
	N	268	270	270	270	177	270
Index Subj3	Pearson Correlation	.000	.115	1	.600**	-.040	.221**
	Sig. (2-tailed)	.996	.060		.000	.600	.000
	N	268	270	270	270	177	270
Index Relig3	Pearson Correlation	.217**	.771**	.600**	1	-.038	.197**
	Sig. (2-tailed)	.000	.000	.000		.612	.001
	N	268	270	270	270	177	270
Index Econ3	Pearson Correlation	.035	-.054	-.040	-.038	1	-.070
	Sig. (2-tailed)	.648	.479	.600	.612		.356
	N	170	177	177	177	178	178
Index Soc7	Pearson Correlation	.013	.103	.221**	.197**	-.070	1
	Sig. (2-tailed)	.834	.092	.000	.001	.356	
	N	268	270	270	270	178	271

**. Correlation is significant at the 0.01 level (2-tailed).

Reference

Descriptive Statistics

	Mean	Std. Deviation	N
Index BibLit	2.7931	.45374	5470
Index Pract3	2.6392	.82213	5473
Index Subj3	1.9831	.69570	5476
Index Relig3	2.4668	.39026	5481
Inbdex Econ3	2.8126	1.00328	3653
Index Soc3	2.1439	.44197	5480

Correlations

		Index BibLit	Index Pract3	Index Subj3	Index Relig3	Index Econ3	Index Soc7
Index BibLit	Pearson Correlation	1	-.143**	-.165**	.141**	.020	-.028*
	Sig. (2-tailed)		.000	.000	.000	.217	.038
	N	5470	5466	5466	5470	3646	5467
Index Pract3	Pearson Correlation	-.143**	1	.179**	.773**	.065**	.052**
	Sig. (2-tailed)	.000		.000	.000	.000	.000
	N	5466	5473	5471	5473	3648	5470
Index Subj3	Pearson Correlation	-.165**	.179**	1	.664**	-.043**	.284**
	Sig. (2-tailed)	.000	.000		.000	.009	.000
	N	5466	5471	5476	5476	3650	5473
Index Relig3	Pearson Correlation	.141**	.773**	.664**	1	.027	.192**
	Sig. (2-tailed)	.000	.000	.000		.108	.000
	N	5470	5473	5476	5481	3652	5478
Index Econ3	Pearson Correlation	.020	.065**	-.043**	.027	1	-.001
	Sig. (2-tailed)	.217	.000	.009	.108		.950
	N	3646	3648	3650	3652	3653	3652
Index Soc7	Pearson Correlation	-.028*	.052**	.284**	.192**	-.001	1
	Sig. (2-tailed)	.038	.000	.000	.000	.950	
	N	5467	5470	5473	5478	3652	5480

**. Correlation is significant at the 0.01 level (2-tailed).
*. Correlation is significant at the 0.05 level (2-tailed).

APPENDIX D.2

PEARSON RHO CORRELATIONS BETWEEN MAIN GROUPS (IGS) AND RELIGIOUS TRADITION FOR DEPENDENT VARIABLES

Immigrants Catholic

Correlations

		Index BibLit	Index Pract3	Index Subj3	Index Relig3	Index Econ3	Index Soc7
Index BibLit	Pearson Correlation	1	-.022	.120*	.448**	-.008	.018
	Sig. (2-tailed)		.704	.041	.000	.913	.761
	N	291	291	291	291	196	291
Index Pract3	Pearson Correlation	.022	1	.087	.741**	-.069	-.060
	Sig. (2-tailed)	.704		.141	.000	.336	.304
	N	291	291	291	291	196	291
Index Subj3	Pearson Correlation	.120*	.087	1	.564**	.068	.077
	Sig. (2-tailed)	.041	.141		.000	.344	.190
	N	291	291	291	291	196	291
Index Relig3	Pearson Correlation	.448**	.741**	.564**	1	-.008	-.006
	Sig. (2-tailed)	.000	.000	.000		.914	.922
	N	291	291	291	291	196	291
Index Econ3	Pearson Correlation	-.008	-.069	.068	-.008	1	.008
	Sig. (2-tailed)	.913	.336	.344	.914		.916
	N	196	196	196	196	196	196
Index Soc7	Pearson Correlation	.018	-.060	.077	-.006	.008	1
	Sig. (2-tailed)	.761	.304	.190	.922	.916	
	N	291	291	291	291	196	291

*. Correlation is significant at the 0.05 level (2-tailed).

**. Correlation is significant at the 0.01 level (2-tailed).

1.5 Generation Catholic

Correlations

		Index BibLit	Index Pract3	Index Subj3	Index Relig3	Index Econ3	Index Soc7
Index BibLit	Pearson Correlation	1	-.151	-.027	.269**	.104	.045
	Sig. (2-tailed)		.129	.789	.006	.369	.655
	N	103	103	103	103	77	102
Index Pract3	Pearson Correlation	-.151	1	.217*	.787**	-.095	.142
	Sig. (2-tailed)	.129		.028	.000	.409	.154
	N	103	103	103	103	77	102
Index Subj3	Pearson Correlation	-.027	.217*	1	.612**	.086	.074
	Sig. (2-tailed)	.789	.028		.000	.460	.461
	N	103	103	103	103	77	102
Index Relig3	Pearson Correlation	.269**	.787**	.612**	1	.034	.136
	Sig. (2-tailed)	.006	.000	.000		.769	.172
	N	103	103	103	103	77	102
Index Econ3	Pearson Correlation	.104	-.095	.086	.034	1	-.012
	Sig. (2-tailed)	.369	.409	.460	.769		.920
	N	77	77	77	77	77	77
Index Soc7	Pearson Correlation	.045	.142	.074	.136	-.012	1
	Sig. (2-tailed)	.655	.154	.461	.172	.920	
	N	102	102	102	102	77	102

**. Correlation is significant at the 0.01 level (2-tailed).
*. Correlation is significant at the 0.05 level (2-tailed).

2nd Generation Catholic

Correlations

		Index BibLit	Index Pract3	Index Subj3	Index Relig3	Index Econ3	Index Soc7
Index BibLit	Pearson Correlation	1	-.004	-.009	.338**	-.078	-.006
	Sig. (2-tailed)		.961	.921	.000	.458	.943
	N	137	137	137	137	92	137
Index Pract3	Pearson Correlation	-.004	1	.105	.861**	-.044	.126
	Sig. (2-tailed)	.961		.224	.000	.676	.143
	N	137	137	137	137	92	137
Index Subj3	Pearson Correlation	-.009	.105	1	.448**	-.177	.156
	Sig. (2-tailed)	.921	.224		.000	.092	.069
	N	137	137	137	137	92	137
Index Relig3	Pearson Correlation	.338**	.861**	.448**	1	-.113	.158
	Sig. (2-tailed)	.000	.000	.000		.285	.066
	N	137	137	137	137	92	137
Index Econ3	Pearson Correlation	-.078	-.044	-.177	-.113	1	.026
	Sig. (2-tailed)	.458	.676	.092	.285		.802
	N	92	92	92	92	92	92
Index Soc7	Pearson Correlation	-.006	.126	.156	.158	.026	1
	Sig. (2-tailed)	.943	.143	.069	.066	.802	
	N	137	137	137	137	92	137

**. Correlation is significant at the 0.01 level (2-tailed).

Reference Catholic

Correlations

		Index BibLit	Index Pract3	Index Subj3	Index Relig3	Index Econ3	Index Soc7
Index BibLit	Pearson Correlation	1	-.108**	-.069*	.238**	.057	-.065*
	Sig. (2-tailed)		.001	.029	.000	.140	.041
	N	998	998	998	998	676	998
Index Pract3	Pearson Correlation	-.108**	1	.062*	.815**	.007	.070*
	Sig. (2-tailed)	.001		.049	.000	.858	.026
	N	998	998	998	998	676	998
Index Subj3	Pearson Correlation	-.069*	.062*	1	.498**	-.008	.158**
	Sig. (2-tailed)	.029	.049		.000	.827	.000
	N	998	998	998	998	676	998
Index Relig3	Pearson Correlation	.238**	.815**	.498**	1	.026	.107**
	Sig. (2-tailed)	.000	.000	.000		.508	.001
	N	998	998	998	998	676	998
Index Econ3	Pearson Correlation	.057	.007	-.008	.026	1	.054
	Sig. (2-tailed)	.140	.858	.827	.508		.162
	N	676	676	676	676	676	676
Index Soc7	Pearson Correlation	-.065*	.070*	.158**	.107**	.054	1
	Sig. (2-tailed)	.041	.026	.000	.001	.162	
	N	998	998	998	998	676	998

**. Correlation is significant at the 0.01 level (2-tailed).
*. Correlation is significant at the 0.05 level (2-tailed).

Immigrant Protestant

Correlations

		Index BibLit	Index Pract3	Index Subj3	Index Relig3	Index Econ3	Index Soc7
Index BibLit	Pearson Correlation	1	-.097	.083	.324**	-.046	.073
	Sig. (2-tailed)		.233	.312	.000	.640	.372
	N	152	152	151	152	105	152
Index Pract3	Pearson Correlation	-.097	1	.050	.777**	.174	-.076
	Sig. (2-tailed)	.233		.542	.000	.076	.350
	N	152	152	151	152	105	152
Index Subj3	Pearson Correlation	.083	.050	1	.536**	.094	.245**
	Sig. (2-tailed)	.312	.542		.000	.343	.002
	N	151	151	151	151	104	151
Index Relig3	Pearson Correlation	.324**	.777**	.536**	1	.146	.096
	Sig. (2-tailed)	.000	.000	.000		.138	.239
	N	152	152	151	152	105	152
Index Econ3	Pearson Correlation	-.046	.174	.094	.146	1	.004
	Sig. (2-tailed)	.640	.076	.343	.138		.964
	N	105	105	104	105	105	105
Index Soc7	Pearson Correlation	.073	-.076	.245**	.096	.004	1
	Sig. (2-tailed)	.372	.350	.002	.239	.964	
	N	152	152	151	152	105	152

**. Correlation is significant at the 0.01 level (2-tailed).

1.5 Generation Protestant

Correlations

		Index BibLit	Index Pract3	Index Subj3	Index Relig3	Index Econ3	Index Soc7
Index BibLit	Pearson Correlation	1	.051	-.113	.389**	-.108	-.096
	Sig. (2-tailed)		.740	.458	.008	.578	.531
	N	45	45	45	45	29	45
Index Pract3	Pearson Correlation	.051	1	-.071	.805**	-.012	-.160
	Sig. (2-tailed)	.740		.644	.000	.951	.294
	N	45	45	45	45	29	45
Index Subj3	Pearson Correlation	-.113	-.071	1	.368*	-.017	.116
	Sig. (2-tailed)	.458	.644		.013	.931	.446
	N	45	45	45	45	29	45
Index Relig3	Pearson Correlation	.389**	.805**	.368*	1	-.033	-.140
	Sig. (2-tailed)	.008	.000	.013		.864	.357
	N	45	45	45	45	29	45
Index Econ3	Pearson Correlation	-.108	-.012	-.017	-.033	1	.155
	Sig. (2-tailed)	.578	.951	.931	.864		.421
	N	29	29	29	29	29	29
Index Soc7	Pearson Correlation	-.096	-.160	.116	-.140	.155	1
	Sig. (2-tailed)	.531	.294	.446	.357	.421	
	N	45	45	45	45	29	45

**. Correlation is significant at the 0.01 level (2-tailed).
*. Correlation is significant at the 0.05 level (2-tailed).

2nd Generation Protestant

Correlations

		Index BibLit	Index Pract3	Index Subj3	Index Relig3	Index Econ3	Index Soc7
Index BibLit	Pearson Correlation	1	.022	.329*	.422**	.166	-.013
	Sig. (2-tailed)		.882	.021	.003	.373	.930
	N	49	49	49	49	31	49
Index Pract3	Pearson Correlation	.022	1	-.165	.820**	.104	.044
	Sig. (2-tailed)	.882		.257	.000	.576	.763
	N	49	49	49	49	31	49
Index Subj3	Pearson Correlation	.329*	-.165	1	.368**	.142	.032
	Sig. (2-tailed)	.021	.257		.009	.445	.825
	N	49	49	49	49	31	49
Index Relig3	Pearson Correlation	.422**	.820**	.368**	1	.206	.058
	Sig. (2-tailed)	.003	.000	.009		.267	.691
	N	49	49	49	49	31	49
Index Econ3	Pearson Correlation	.166	.104	.142	.206	1	-.398*
	Sig. (2-tailed)	.373	.576	.445	.267		.027
	N	31	31	31	31	31	31
Index Soc7	Pearson Correlation	-.013	.044	.032	.058	-.398*	1
	Sig. (2-tailed)	.930	.763	.825	.691	.027	
	N	49	49	49	49	31	49

*. Correlation is significant at the 0.05 level (2-tailed).
**. Correlation is significant at the 0.01 level (2-tailed).

Appendix D.2

Reference Protestant

Correlations

		Index BibLit	Index Pract3	Index Subj3	Index Relig3	Index Econ3	Index Soc7
Index BibLit	Pearson Correlation	1	-.049[**]	.014	.317[**]	.010	.038[*]
	Sig. (2-tailed)		.006	.425	.000	.655	.033
	N	3135	3134	3134	3135	2087	3132
Index Pract3	Pearson Correlation	-.049[**]	1	-.029	.790[**]	.097[**]	-.035
	Sig. (2-tailed)	.006		.101	.000	.000	.051
	N	3134	3137	3136	3137	2088	3134
Index Subj3	Pearson Correlation	.014	-.029	1	.470[**]	-.006	.271[**]
	Sig. (2-tailed)	.425	.101		.000	.780	.000
	N	3134	3136	3139	3139	2089	3136
Index Relig3	Pearson Correlation	.317[**]	.790[**]	.470[**]	1	.083[**]	.119[**]
	Sig. (2-tailed)	.000	.000	.000		.000	.000
	N	3135	3137	3139	3140	2089	3137
Index Econ3	Pearson Correlation	.010	.097[**]	-.006	.083[**]	1	-.028
	Sig. (2-tailed)	.655	.000	.780	.000		.193
	N	2087	2088	2089	2089	2089	2088
Index Soc7	Pearson Correlation	.038[*]	-.035	.271[**]	.119[**]	-.028	1
	Sig. (2-tailed)	.033	.051	.000	.000	.193	
	N	3132	3134	3136	3137	2088	3137

**. Correlation is significant at the 0.01 level (2-tailed).
*. Correlation is significant at the 0.05 level (2-tailed).

APPENDIX D.3

PEARSON RHO CORRELATIONS BETWEEN MAIN GROUPS (IGS) AND GENDER FOR DEPENDENT VARIABLES

Immigrant Male

Correlations

		Index BibLit	Index Pract3	Index Subj3	Index Relig3	Index Econ3	Index Soc7
Index BibLit	Pearson Correlation	1	-.121*	-.211**	.197**	-.005	-.006
	Sig. (2-tailed)		.045	.000	.001	.945	.927
	N	277	277	276	277	179	277
Index Pract3	Pearson Correlation	-.121*	1	.258**	.805**	.113	.054
	Sig. (2-tailed)	.045		.000	.000	.132	.372
	N	277	278	277	278	179	278
Index Subj3	Pearson Correlation	-.211**	.258**	1	.619**	.080	.129*
	Sig. (2-tailed)	.000	.000		.000	.289	.032
	N	276	277	277	277	178	277
Index Relig3	Pearson Correlation	.197**	.805**	.619**	1	.110	.109
	Sig. (2-tailed)	.001	.000	.000		.141	.071
	N	277	278	277	278	179	278
Index Econ3	Pearson Correlation	-.005	.113	.080	.110	1	.029
	Sig. (2-tailed)	.945	.132	.289	.141		.696
	N	179	179	178	179	179	179
Index Soc7	Pearson Correlation	-.006	.054	.129*	.109	.029	1
	Sig. (2-tailed)	.927	.372	.032	.071	.696	
	N	277	278	277	278	179	279

*. Correlation is significant at the 0.05 level (2-tailed).

**. Correlation is significant at the 0.01 level (2-tailed).

1.5 Generation Male

Correlations

		Index BibLit	Index Pract3	Index Subj3	Index Relig3	Index Econ3	Index Soc7
Index BibLit	Pearson Correlation	1	-.241*	-.084	.133	.052	.024
	Sig. (2-tailed)		.020	.422	.205	.681	.821
	N	93	93	93	93	66	92
Index Pract3	Pearson Correlation	-.241*	1	.312**	.766**	.054	.101
	Sig. (2-tailed)	.020		.002	.000	.667	.339
	N	93	93	93	93	66	92
Index Subj3	Pearson Correlation	-.084	.312**	1	.746**	.160	.048
	Sig. (2-tailed)	.422	.002		.000	.199	.648
	N	93	93	93	93	66	92
Index Relig3	Pearson Correlation	.133	.766**	.746**	1	.167	.086
	Sig. (2-tailed)	.205	.000	.000		.180	.418
	N	93	93	93	93	66	92
Index Econ3	Pearson Correlation	.052	.054	.160	.167	1	-.007
	Sig. (2-tailed)	.681	.667	.199	.180		.954
	N	66	66	66	66	66	66
Index Soc7	Pearson Correlation	.024	.101	.048	.086	-.007	1
	Sig. (2-tailed)	.821	.339	.648	.418	.954	
	N	92	92	92	92	66	92

*. Correlation is significant at the 0.05 level (2-tailed).
**. Correlation is significant at the 0.01 level (2-tailed).

2nd Generation Male

Correlations

		Index BibLit	Index Pract3	Index Subj3	Index Relig3	Index Econ3	Index Soc7
Index BibLit	Pearson Correlation	1	-.188	-.206*	.071	.212	-.027
	Sig. (2-tailed)		.050	.032	.466	.074	.782
	N	109	109	109	109	72	109
Index Pract3	Pearson Correlation	-.188	1	.221*	.835**	.047	.079
	Sig. (2-tailed)	.050		.021	.000	.695	.417
	N	109	109	109	109	72	109
Index Subj3	Pearson Correlation	-.206*	.221*	1	.611**	-.081	.176
	Sig. (2-tailed)	.032	.021		.000	.499	.067
	N	109	109	109	109	72	109
Index Relig3	Pearson Correlation	.071	.835**	.611**	1	.072	.144
	Sig. (2-tailed)	.466	.000	.000		.548	.135
	N	109	109	109	109	72	109
Index Econ3	Pearson Correlation	.212	.047	-.081	.072	1	-.051
	Sig. (2-tailed)	.074	.695	.499	.548		.669
	N	72	72	72	72	73	73
Index Soc7	Pearson Correlation	-.027	.079	.176	.144	-.051	1
	Sig. (2-tailed)	.782	.417	.067	.135	.669	
	N	109	109	109	109	73	110

*. Correlation is significant at the 0.05 level (2-tailed).
**. Correlation is significant at the 0.01 level (2-tailed).

Reference Male

Correlations

		Index BibLit	Index Pract3	Index Subj3	Index Relig3	Index Econ3	Index Soc7
Index BibLit	Pearson Correlation	1	-.146**	-.211**	.128**	.029	-.016
	Sig. (2-tailed)		.000	.000	.000	.246	.424
	N	2415	2414	2414	2415	1603	2415
Index Pract3	Pearson Correlation	-.146**	1	.258**	.786**	.041	.040*
	Sig. (2-tailed)	.000		.000	.000	.097	.047
	N	2414	2419	2418	2419	1606	2419
Index Subj3	Pearson Correlation	-.211**	.258**	1	.691**	-.067**	.265**
	Sig. (2-tailed)	.000	.000		.000	.007	.000
	N	2414	2418	2423	2423	1608	2423
Index Relig3	Pearson Correlation	.128**	.786**	.691**	1	-.004	.178**
	Sig. (2-tailed)	.000	.000	.000		.867	.000
	N	2415	2419	2423	2424	1608	2424
Index Econ3	Pearson Correlation	.029	.041	-.067**	-.004	1	-.012
	Sig. (2-tailed)	.246	.097	.007	.867		.618
	N	1603	1606	1608	1608	1609	1609
Index Soc7	Pearson Correlation	-.016	.040*	.265**	.178**	-.012	1
	Sig. (2-tailed)	.424	.047	.000	.000	.618	
	N	2415	2419	2423	2424	1609	2426

**. Correlation is significant at the 0.01 level (2-tailed).
*. Correlation is significant at the 0.05 level (2-tailed).

Immigrant Female

Correlations

		Index BibLit	Index Pract3	Index Subj3	Index Relig3	Index Econ3	Index Soc7
Index BibLit	Pearson Correlation	1	-.197**	.103	.312**	-.028	-.047
	Sig. (2-tailed)		.000	.064	.000	.678	.402
	N	324	324	323	324	221	324
Index Pract3	Pearson Correlation	-.197**	1	.070	.681**	.046	.028
	Sig. (2-tailed)	.000		.208	.000	.492	.617
	N	324	325	324	325	221	325
Index Subj3	Pearson Correlation	.103	.070	1	.639**	.030	.189**
	Sig. (2-tailed)	.064	.208		.000	.662	.001
	N	323	324	324	324	221	324
Index Relig3	Pearson Correlation	.312**	.681**	.639**	1	.049	.113*
	Sig. (2-tailed)	.000	.000	.000		.472	.041
	N	324	325	324	325	221	325
Index Econ3	Pearson Correlation	-.028	.046	.030	.049	1	-.019
	Sig. (2-tailed)	.678	.492	.662	.472		.784
	N	221	221	221	221	221	221
Index Soc7	Pearson Correlation	-.047	.028	.189**	.113*	-.019	1
	Sig. (2-tailed)	.402	.617	.001	.041	.784	
	N	324	325	324	325	221	325

**. Correlation is significant at the 0.01 level (2-tailed).
*. Correlation is significant at the 0.05 level (2-tailed).

1.5 Generation Female

Correlations

		Index BibLit	Index Pract3	Index Subj3	Index Relig3	Index Econ3	Index Soc7
Index BibLit	Pearson Correlation	1	.050	-.203*	.222*	.054	.004
	Sig. (2-tailed)		.596	.029	.017	.638	.962
	N	115	115	115	115	78	115
Index Pract3	Pearson Correlation	.050	1	.198*	.776**	-.123	-.105
	Sig. (2-tailed)	.596		.033	.000	.284	.264
	N	115	116	116	116	78	116
Index Subj3	Pearson Correlation	-.203*	.198*	1	.669**	-.110	.173
	Sig. (2-tailed)	.029	.033		.000	.336	.063
	N	115	116	116	116	78	116
Index Relig3	Pearson Correlation	.222*	.776**	.669**	1	-.131	.052
	Sig. (2-tailed)	.017	.000	.000		.253	.583
	N	115	116	116	116	78	116
Index Econ3	Pearson Correlation	.054	-.123	-.110	-.131	1	.179
	Sig. (2-tailed)	.638	.284	.336	.253		.116
	N	78	78	78	78	78	78
Index Soc7	Pearson Correlation	.004	-.105	.173	.052	.179	1
	Sig. (2-tailed)	.962	.264	.063	.583	.116	
	N	115	116	116	116	78	116

2nd Generation Female

Correlations

		Index BibLit	Index Pract3	Index Subj3	Index Relig3	Index Econ3	Index Soc7
Index BibLit	Pearson Correlation	1	-.155	.137	.323**	-.052	.070
	Sig. (2-tailed)		.051	.084	.000	.599	.381
	N	159	159	159	159	104	159
Index Pract3	Pearson Correlation	-.155	1	.031	.730**	-.161	.089
	Sig. (2-tailed)	.051		.697	.000	.100	.260
	N	159	161	161	161	105	161
Index Subj3	Pearson Correlation	.137	.031	1	.587**	-.021	.236**
	Sig. (2-tailed)	.084	.697		.000	.832	.003
	N	159	161	161	161	105	161
Index Relig3	Pearson Correlation	.323**	.730**	.587**	1	-.144	.216**
	Sig. (2-tailed)	.000	.000	.000		.144	.006
	N	159	161	161	161	105	161
Index Econ3	Pearson Correlation	-.052	-.161	-.021	-.144	1	-.121
	Sig. (2-tailed)	.599	.100	.832	.144		.220
	N	104	105	105	105	105	105
Index Soc7	Pearson Correlation	.070	.089	.236**	.216**	-.121	1
	Sig. (2-tailed)	.381	.260	.003	.006	.220	
	N	159	161	161	161	105	161

**. Correlation is significant at the 0.01 level (2-tailed).

Reference Female

Correlations

		Index BibLit	Index Pract3	Index Subj3	Index Relig3	Index Econ3	Index Soc7
Index BibLit	Pearson Correlation	1	-.119**	-.097**	.190**	.026	-.017
	Sig. (2-tailed)		.000	.000	.000	.239	.360
	N	3055	3052	3052	3055	2043	3052
Index Pract3	Pearson Correlation	-.119**	1	.074**	.754**	.062**	.028
	Sig. (2-tailed)	.000		.000	.000	.005	.124
	N	3052	3054	3053	3054	2042	3051
Index Subj3	Pearson Correlation	-.097**	.074**	1	.620**	-.052*	.271**
	Sig. (2-tailed)	.000	.000		.000	.019	.000
	N	3052	3053	3053	3053	2042	3050
Index Relig3	Pearson Correlation	.190**	.754**	.620**	1	.025	.169**
	Sig. (2-tailed)	.000	.000	.000		.267	.000
	N	3055	3054	3053	3057	2044	3054
Index Econ3	Pearson Correlation	.026	.062**	-.052*	.025	1	-.013
	Sig. (2-tailed)	.239	.005	.019	.267		.545
	N	2043	2042	2042	2044	2044	2043
Index Soc7	Pearson Correlation	-.017	.028	.271**	.169**	-.013	1
	Sig. (2-tailed)	.360	.124	.000	.000	.545	
	N	3052	3051	3050	3054	2043	3054

**. Correlation is significant at the 0.01 level (2-tailed).

*. Correlation is significant at the 0.05 level (2-tailed).

APPENDIX E.1

DEMOGRAPHIC PROFILE
FOR MAIN GROUPS (IGS)

Gender	Immigrant	1.5	2	Reference	Grand Total
Count	604	209	271	5483	6567
Female	53.8%	55.5%	59.4%	55.8%	55.4%
Male	46.2%	44.5%	40.6%	44.2%	44.0%

Years of Education	Immigrant	1.5	2	Reference	Grand Total
Count	604	209	271	5483	6567
1 to 6	17.2%	7.2%	1.8%	1.0%	2.7%
7 to 11	16.9%	15.3%	17.0%	13.1%	13.6%
12	14.6%	26.3%	24.4%	28.6%	26.9%
13 to 15	18.4%	30.6%	28.0%	27.7%	26.8%
16	13.7%	12.0%	10.1%	16.1%	15.7%
17+	16.1%	8.6%	10.7%	13.2%	13.2%

Age Bracket	Immigrant	1.5	2	Reference	Grand Total
Count	604	209	271	5483	6567
18-24	5.0%	16.3%	16.6%	8.4%	8.6%
25-34	24.0%	34.9%	21.0%	16.5%	17.9%
35-44	27.0%	24.9%	12.5%	18.5%	19.1%
45-54	18.4%	11.5%	8.5%	20.7%	19.6%
55-64	10.4%	7.7%	8.1%	17.4%	15.9%
65-74	8.9%	2.9%	8.9%	10.8%	10.2%
75+	4.8%	1.9%	23.6%	6.6%	6.9%

Marital Staus	Immigrant	1.5	2	Reference	Grand Total
Count	604	209	271	5483	6567
Married	57.3%	46.9%	35.1%	46.2%	46.5%
Never married	20.9%	37.8%	33.9%	25.3%	25.5%
Divorced	8.9%	10.0%	9.6%	17.0%	15.6%
Separated	7.8%	3.8%	3.0%	3.0%	3.4%
Widowed	5.1%	1.4%	18.1%	8.5%	8.3%

APPENDIX E.2

DEMOGRAPHIC PROFILE FOR MAIN GROUPS (IGS) BY RELIGIOUS TRADITION (PROTESTANT)

Count	152	45	49	3140	3386
Gender	Immigrant	1.5	2	Reference	Grand Total
Female	59.2%	52.0%	68.9%	59.2%	59.0%
Male	40.8%	48.0%	31.1%	40.8%	41.0%
Years of Education	Immigrant	1.5	2	Reference	Grand Total
1 to 6	2.0%	16.4%	2.2%	1.3%	2.0%
7 to 11	20.4%	17.1%	11.1%	14.4%	14.6%
12	22.4%	13.2%	24.4%	30.1%	29.1%
13 to 15	24.5%	17.1%	42.2%	27.3%	27.0%
16	16.3%	16.4%	13.3%	15.1%	15.2%
17+	14.3%	15.8%	6.7%	11.5%	11.6%
Mean	12.0	13.2	13.4	13.4	13.2
Std. Dev.	5.0	3.0	3.3	2.8	3.0
Age Bracket	Immigrant	1.5	2	Reference	Grand Total
18-24	14.3%	4.6%	22.2%	5.9%	6.1%
25-34	18.4%	17.1%	26.7%	14.2%	14.5%
35-44	10.2%	23.7%	26.7%	17.7%	18.0%
45-54	12.2%	19.1%	11.1%	21.5%	21.1%
55-64	14.3%	14.5%	4.4%	18.7%	18.2%
65-74	12.2%	10.5%	2.2%	12.2%	12.0%
75+	16.3%	9.2%	6.7%	8.4%	8.5%
Mean	48.9	37.4	50.6	50.6	50.3
Std. Dev.	17.1	15.8	21.4	17.0	17.1
Marital Staus	Immigrant	1.5	2	Reference	Grand Total
Married	51.1%	36.7%	53.9%	49.3%	49.4%
Never married	37.8%	36.7%	18.4%	19.3%	19.8%
Divorced	4.4%	6.1%	9.2%	17.4%	16.7%
Separated	37.8%	36.7%	18.4%	19.3%	19.8%
Widowed	2.2%	0.0%	8.6%	3.4%	3.6%

Appendix E.2

DEMOGRAPHIC PROFILE
FOR MAIN GROUPS (IGS)
BY RELIGIOUS TRADITION (CATHOLIC)

Count	291	103	137	998	1529
Gender	Immigrant	1.5	2	Reference	Grand Total
Female	49.5%	57.7%	59.5%	57.5%	57.4%
Male	50.5%	42.3%	40.5%	42.5%	42.6%
Years of Education	Immigrant	1.5	2	Reference	Grand Total
1 to 6	25.4%	9.7%	2.2%	0.5%	6.0%
7 to 11	21.3%	18.4%	19.0%	8.1%	12.3%
12	17.2%	33.0%	26.3%	29.3%	26.9%
13 to 15	16.2%	25.2%	29.2%	28.8%	26.2%
16	9.6%	9.7%	16.8%	17.7%	15.6%
17+	7.2%	3.9%	6.6%	15.4%	12.3%
Mean	10.4	11.9	13.2	14.0	13.1
Std. Dev.	4.7	3.2	2.7	2.7	3.5
Age Bracket	Immigrant	1.5	2	Reference	Grand Total
18-24	5.2%	15.5%	19.0%	9.0%	9.6%
25-34	24.7%	36.9%	19.0%	14.9%	18.6%
35-44	27.5%	24.3%	13.9%	18.4%	20.1%
45-54	17.9%	9.7%	7.3%	20.5%	18.1%
55-64	10.3%	7.8%	8.0%	17.2%	14.5%
65-74	8.9%	4.9%	7.3%	12.0%	10.5%
75+	3.4%	1.0%	24.8%	7.0%	7.5%
Mean	44.8	36.8	48.8	48.6	47.1
Std. Dev.	15.2	14.0	23.3	17.2	17.6
Marital Staus	Immigrant	1.5	2	Reference	Grand Total
Married	57.0%	40.8%	37.2%	48.8%	48.8%
Never married	20.3%	42.7%	29.2%	25.4%	25.9%
Divorced	7.9%	10.7%	10.2%	15.8%	13.5%
Separated	10.0%	4.9%	3.6%	1.4%	3.5%
Widowed	4.8%	1.0%	19.7%	8.6%	8.4%

APPENDIX E.3

DEMOGRAPHIC PROFILE
FOR MAIN GROUPS (IGS) BY FEMALE GENDER

Years of Education	Immigrant	1.5	2	Reference	Grand Total
Count	325	116	161	3057	3659
1 to 6	16.9%	6.0%	0.6%	1.1%	2.7%
7 to 11	14.2%	16.4%	18.6%	12.3%	12.9%
12	15.4%	27.6%	23.6%	29.3%	27.8%
13 to 15	20.6%	30.2%	29.8%	29.0%	28.4%
16	15.4%	11.2%	19.3%	14.9%	15.1%
17+	13.5%	8.6%	8.1%	13.0%	12.7%

Age Bracket	Immigrant	1.5	2	Reference	Grand Total
Count	325	116	161	3057	3659
18-24	4.6%	14.7%	14.3%	8.5%	8.6%
25-34	24.6%	31.9%	22.4%	17.0%	18.4%
35-44	28.3%	27.6%	13.7%	18.2%	19.2%
45-54	17.2%	12.9%	6.8%	19.8%	18.7%
55-64	10.8%	7.8%	8.1%	16.3%	15.2%
65-74	7.1%	3.4%	10.6%	11.2%	10.5%
75+	5.5%	1.7%	23.6%	7.6%	7.9%

Marital Staus	Immigrant	1.5	2	Reference	Grand Total
Count	325	116	161	3057	3659
Married	50.9%	34.8%	54.8%	44.1%	44.8%
Never married	31.0%	29.2%	18.2%	23.1%	23.2%
Divorced	11.2%	9.9%	8.9%	17.2%	15.9%
Separated	5.2%	3.1%	8.9%	3.2%	3.7%
Widowed	1.7%	22.4%	9.2%	12.4%	12.2%

Appendix E.3

DEMOGRAPHIC PROFILE
FOR MAIN GROUPS (IGS) BY MALE GENDER

Years of Education	Immigrant	1.5	2	Reference	Grand Total
Count	279	93	110	2426	2908
1 to 6	8.6%	17.6%	17.6%	0.9%	2.8%
7 to 11	14.0%	20.1%	20.1%	14.1%	14.6%
12	24.7%	13.6%	13.6%	27.7%	26.2%
13 to 15	31.2%	15.8%	15.8%	26.0%	25.1%
16	12.9%	11.8%	11.8%	17.6%	16.8%
17+	8.6%	19.0%	19.0%	13.6%	14.0%

Age Bracket	Immigrant	1.5	2	Reference	Grand Total
Count	279	93	110	2426	2908
18-24	20.0%	5.4%	18.3%	8.2%	8.7%
25-34	19.1%	23.3%	38.7%	16.0%	17.5%
35-44	10.9%	25.4%	21.5%	18.8%	19.2%
45-54	10.9%	19.7%	9.7%	21.9%	20.9%
55-64	8.2%	10.0%	7.5%	18.7%	17.1%
65-74	6.4%	11.1%	2.2%	10.3%	10.0%
75+	23.6%	3.9%	2.2%	5.4%	5.8%

Marital Staus	Immigrant	1.5	2	Reference	Grand Total
Count	279	93	110	2426	2908
Married	60.2%	41.9%	35.5%	48.9%	49.2%
Never married	24.0%	46.2%	40.9%	27.9%	28.0%
Divorced	0.0%	0.0%	0.0%	0.1%	0.1%
Separated	6.5%	2.2%	2.7%	2.8%	3.1%
Widowed	0.4%	1.1%	11.8%	3.6%	3.5%